Changing people's lives for the better

RABBI ZELIG PLISKIN

KINDNESS

published by

ARTSCROLL

SHAAR PRESS

Changing people's lives for the better

RABBI ZELIG PLISKIN

TABLE OF CONTENTS

INTRODUCTION

Developing a love for kindness transforms your life as you transform the lives of others. Kindness is one of the pillars of the world. Every act of kindness elevates your character and makes you a kinder person. As you continue to increase your love for kindness, you increase the amount of joy in your life.

There are minor acts of kindness and major acts of kindness. Every kind deed and word is precious and valuable. Every kind deed and word is eternal. And when your actions and words have a positive lifetime effect on someone, you have created something magnificent, whether or not the extent of its greatness is recognized by any other mortal.

As you expand your consciousness of kindness, you create a more spiritual life. Your kindness and compassion for the Creator's children is an expression of your love for our Father, our King, Creator and Sustainer of the universe. With your kindness and compassion you emulate Him. As you help others, you create an inner light that illuminates your entire being.

A master artist looks at an entirely different world than someone who lacks his vision. We can all train ourselves to see more deeply. When you see the world as a place in which to do kindness, you see a different world. You see a world full of spiritual opportunities wherever you are and wherever you go. Let this be your world.

I am grateful to all those who have made a difference in my life and have taught me the meaning of kindness. I am especially grateful to my father, of blessed memory, and my mother, may she be well.

I wish to express my gratitude to Reb Shmuel Blitz of ArtScroll and the entire ArtScroll staff for all that they have done to make this book possible. I am deeply grateful to Rabbi Noah Weinberg, whose kindness has made a major difference to so many. And I express my thanks to Rabbi Kalman Packouz for his ongoing encouragement and kindness.

Words cannot express my profound gratitude to my brother-in-law Rabbi Hershel Weinberg for his self-sacrificing kindness.

I

MAKING A DIFFERENCE IN PEOPLE'S LIVES

"I felt that I was wasting my life. My family was financially secure. We had a nice home and were considered prosperous by our community. But I didn't feel that I was living a meaningful life. A deep feeling of emptiness gnawed at me. I analyzed my life situation and compared it with the lives of others whom I respected. What was the difference? Those I admired all made a significant contribution to the welfare of others. Each did this in a unique way. But the common denominator was that they all did things that made a difference in people's lives. I made a sincere commitment to do the same. That was over 10 years ago and words are inadequate to describe the difference this has made in my life.

"What can I say or do to make a difference in this person's life?" This is the question that, when asked, consistently elevates one's character.

There are unlimited ways to make a difference. This can be done with our time, energy, money, possessions, food, understanding, listening, advice, knowledge, and the list goes on and on.

One of the great developers of character in our generation, Rabbi Shlomo Wolbe, has frequently said that the first step to becoming a kind person is to be aware of the specific needs of each person you encounter. "What is this person missing?" is the question which must come to mind.

"It might sound easy," he wrote. "But as soon as you try to do this you will see how difficult it really is."

When someone tells you explicitly what's bothering him, this is a straightforward process. But often a person will not tell you. He has no reason to assume that you can or are willing to help him. Perhaps this is your first encounter. The person is a stranger and your sensitivity to his needs will turn him into a friend. Some people are shy or proud and don't feel comfortable turning to others. At times a person might not even know himself what he is lacking and what he really needs to enhance his life.

Our goal is to become experts at discovering people's needs so that we will be able to read between the lines when we listen to their dialogue. We will be able to read people's faces and hear the nuances in their tone of voice. Like all skills, this takes considerable practice over a long period of time.

This book is intended as a manual on how to make a difference in the lives of other people. As you master this art, your own life will be elevated and enriched. You will know that your own life has meaning and significance. The benefits you will reap will be everlasting.

2.

A FEW SECONDS THAT LAST FOREVER

A kind word can last forever. An encouraging word can be the foundation upon which many constructive years will be established. Enhancing the self-image of a child with a brief but powerful comment can create a magnificent human being. Words that inspire are like the fuel that enables the rocket to fly high and far.

Will every kind word be remembered? Not always consciously. But it's there in one's subconscious. The recipient of that kind word is likely to pass it on to others. So your words of kindness can be like an eternal chain or a perpetual motion machine.

It might take you a few seconds to encourage someone who is about to give up. That person has the potential to have a major impact on many lives. Those future accomplishments might not have happened if not for your words of encouragement.

When your words are intended to uplift, to encourage, to influence, to motivate, to inspire, be aware that what you say can endure for many years. The ensuing benefits can help multitudes of individuals and families for many generations. Your words are powerful. Use them wisely.

Rabbi Yisrael Salanter, the founder of a major approach to spiritual growth and self-development, attributed all he accomplished in life to one sentence he heard from Rabbi Zundel of Salant. Similarly, the Alter of Navardok heard one sentence from Rabbi Yisrael Salanter that made him think about what kind of person he wanted to be in the future. Everyone reading this and similar works is among the many others who are the heirs to the spiritual benefits of that original one sentence.

I have a friend who was not using his full potential in school. His teacher convinced his parents to send him to a school that motivated its students to reach their potential. That 10-minute conversation led to his succeeding beyond his parents' wildest dreams.

As I was writing this book, a neighbor told me, "Recently someone reminded me that I gave him encouragement when he was going through a major crisis. He had serious thoughts of ending his life. My friendly care and concern gave him the strength not to do anything drastic. That was over 20 years ago. He is forever grateful for the life that I enabled him to live."

3

JOY FOR KINDNESS

E xperiencing joy for doing acts of kindness for others will increase the quantity and quality of your kind acts. When you enjoy doing things to help others, you will always be able to find enjoyable things to do. The life of a person who loves to do acts of kindness will be a life of joy.

You may reason that it's selfish to feel joyous for helping others. Put yourself in the position of the recipient of kind deeds or words. Wouldn't you prefer that the people who are kind to you feel good about what they accomplish? Compare the following thoughts that might be going through the mind of someone who is doing something to help you.

"I hate wasting my time with this person. Why is he bothering me? Why can't he just leave me alone. I can't wait until he gets out of here."

— or —

"I love to spend my time helping this person. I'm so glad that

he asked me to assist him. I feel so good about being able to do acts of kindness that I hope he asks me another time."

Of course, we all feel better when people who goes out of their way to help us enjoy what they are doing.

What if you don't spontaneously feel joy for the kind acts that you do? Think of the positive spiritual effects your words and actions have on you. Be aware of how you are elevating yourself and becoming a better person. Imagine the good feelings you would have if someone helped you in the way that you are helping this person. By entering his world and feeling what he is feeling you gain a greater appreciation for what you are doing. Some people find this easier to do than others. But as you begin to experience this even a tiny bit, you are increasing your ability to do so.

Imagine feeling intense joy. Think of an event, a situation, or an occurrence that would make you feel really great. See what you would see, hear what you would hear, and feel what you would feel. Now increase the intensity of what you would see, hear, and feel. Allow yourself to access these feelings when you do acts of kindness. If you aren't able to do this at first, keep trying. Your persistence will eventually enable you to experience increased joy for doing acts of kindness.

I once met a person who seemed extremely happy every time he did an act of kindness.

"Did your joy for doing kindness come naturally to you?" I asked him.

"Definitely not," he replied. "If my joy came naturally I don't think it would be as strong as it is now. I have to admit that I really am selfish and I have to make a concerted effort to create a joyous attitude. What worked for me was the thought, 'If I just won a major international lottery how would I react?' I would celebrate with my entire being and would be extremely excited and euphoric. I vividly paint a mental picture of my hearing the great news. Then I think of how the value of kindness is even greater than winning a lottery. This intense joy becomes associated in my mind with doing kindness. Now my joy is automatic and I don't need to do anything special to create it."

4

THERE IS A REASON YOU ARE THERE

Wherever you are, you are there for a reason. There are times when the reason will be patently evident. At other times you will need to be patient to understand why. Having a kindness consciousness will enable you to understand seemingly puzzling occurrences. The less you want to be in a certain place, the more you should be on the lookout for opportunities to make a difference in someone's life.

I usually take just one bus to go home from work. One day I impulsively took a different bus and needed a second bus to take me to a third bus which would get me home. On the second bus I overheard a conversation between two people sitting directly behind me. One of the gentlemen was describing how lost he felt in life. His life lacked meaning. I wasn't certain if I should get involved. Shortly before I left the bus, I spoke up. What I was able to suggest made the entire trip worthwhile, for both of us.

The flight I was scheduled to be on was overbooked, and I was put on the next plane going to my destination. The man who sat near me asked my help in solving a difficult dilemma concerning his professional career. When I said good-bye to him, he commented, "I'll probably never see you again. But this short encounter has made you a major person in my life." That was why I had to wait for so many hours at the airport.

I missed my car ride and on the way to the bus stop I met a stranger in town who was totally lost. Because I was there at that moment, I was able to provide him with accurate directions.

I mistakenly showed up for a wedding on the wrong day. At the wedding hall, I met an acquaintance who also made a similar mistake. He felt like a total fool. I was glad that my making the same mistake made him feel so much better.

I was scheduled to give a lecture. The newspaper ad printed the date incorrectly. I showed up on the incorrect date to personally apologize for the error. I had a long conversation with one individual as to how he could create a better relationship with his son. That conversation would not have taken place if I wouldn't have made that effort. What might have seemed like a waste of time to rectify the printer's error, turned out to be an opportunity to help a family for many years to come.

The store had unexpectedly long lines that day. While chatting with a man waiting in front of me, I suggested a job opportunity that proved to be beneficial.

Only one man showed up for my lecture. Instead of a formal class, we had a fascinating discussion. This man was a physician with an ingenious ability to diagnose and heal. I knew three people who could use his healing talents. It was fortunate for everyone concerned that no one else showed up, for we forged a lasting friendship that was helpful to many individuals.

5.

YOUR IDENTITY

Your identity has a tremendous influence on your behavior. What we do readily or refuse to do is strongly connected with how we identify who we are. We tend to say, "I'll do that. That's who I am." Or, "I would never think of doing that. I'm not that kind of person." This pattern can work for us or against us, depending on the nature of our subjective identity.

There was a famous study designed to illustrate the power of our sense of identity.

"Can we place this large billboard with the words DRIVE CAREFULLY on your front lawn?" a number of homeowners were asked. Unbeknown to them the question was posed by a student working on a research project.

Understandably, most people answered, "No." They didn't want unsightly signs on their expensive front lawns.

This same request was then posed in two steps. The homeowners were asked, "Are you for safe driving?" Everyone replied, "Of course, yes."

"Then would you please sign this petition for safe driving." Most agreed to sign.

Several weeks later those who signed were approached again. "You signed a declaration that you are for safe driving. Are you still for safe driving today?"

"Yes. I haven't changed my mind," was the unanimous response.

"Since you are a person who cares about safe driving, could you please allow us to place this billboard with a DRIVE CARE-FULLY message on your front lawn?"

Most agreed. Why? Because once they identified themselves as individuals who cared about safe driving, they acted consistently with their new identity. Previously, even if they agreed, they might have done so reluctantly. Now that they were acting in a way consistent with their identity as being concerned about safe driving, they felt good about doing their part to help save lives. This principle applies in all areas.

On our subject, the principle can be stated in this way: Identify yourself as a person who is kind and caring and you will spontaneously upgrade your level of kindness.

There are many instances when you will have opportunities to do acts of kindness for others but might not be open to do them. At times you might not recognize the opportunity. At other times, you just won't feel like doing the kind deed. Or you might not feel that it's important for you to speak up.

When you identify yourself as a person who loves kindness, you will notice opportunities you hadn't noticed before. You will feel like doing acts of kindness you didn't feel like doing before.

And you will always feel that it's up to you to do as much good as you can throughout your life.

As you develop your love for kindness, you will view yourself as a person with a life goal to help others. You might not choose to share this identity with others, but in your heart you will know that this is who you are.

WHAT KIND OF PERSON ARE YOU?

With each action you take and with every word you say, you answer an important question. "What kind of person are you?"

Are you a giver or a taker? All takers must give and all givers must take. But there is a basic pattern of giving and a basic pattern of taking. A giver thinks about what he can do for others. He takes in order to give. A taker thinks about what others can do for him. Even when he gives, it is only because he wants to take. By increasing your giving, you become more of a giver.

Are you a person who loves to do acts of kindness? You answer this by the way you react when people ask you to do things for them. Are you pleased to have opportunities to help others or do you resent people bothering you? The more you increase your sense of joy for doing things for others, the more you become a lover of kindness.

As you respond compassionately to the plight of others, you become a compassionate person. Ignoring the plight of others gives a very different answer to the question, "What kind of person are you?"

When you go beyond the ordinary to do major things for another human being, you create an extraordinary person. There is no limit to the heights to which you can elevate yourself.

When you spend time thinking of creative ways to help others, your creativity is a work of art. There are many forms of creative artistry. The form that elevates you the most is creative kindness. You look for ways to help people who need help but are reluctant to take anything — even time — from others. You find creative ways to cheer up the despondent, to help people overcome their obstacles, and to make peace between people who quarrel. As you creatively find answers to people's problems, the person you become is an elevated creative artist. You are creating a better life for a fellow human being.

What kind of person do you really want to be? Writing this in the form of a mission statement or an essay has a powerful effect on one's self-image. The act of writing that you want to be a kind and compassionate giver motivates positive action. And the question "What kind of person are you?" is actually answered by the way you speak to others and what you do for them.

YOU ARE UNIQUE

Every kind person is unique. You have unique talents, skills, knowledge, and resources. Utilize them to help others in ways that are uniquely yours. Learn from other kind people, but don't compare yourself with anyone else. Others will be able to do things that you cannot. And you will be able to do things that others cannot.

One who sings well can utilize this talent to cheer up the despondent, the ill, and those who need an emotional lift. One who has been blessed with financial wealth can help those who lack the means to meet their needs. One with time and energy can volunteer to help the elderly and those who require physical assistance. One with life experience can share the expertise amassed over time with those who will benefit.

A younger person will be able to help out in ways that an older person cannot. And an older person will be able to help out in a way that a younger person cannot. A professional will be able to help out in certain ways and a layman will be able to help out in other ways. At times one's lack of resources is exactly what will render him more effective in a particular situation.

Don't let the feeling that others are doing more than you, discourage you from doing good. First of all, you can never tell how much a seemingly small act of yours has accomplished.

Furthermore, you might have an opportunity to do a major act of kindness for an individual or an entire group of people. Opportunities for kindness can present themselves in unexpected ways. And it is because you will be the right person at the right place at the right time that will make a major difference. So keep your focus on what you can do rather than on what anyone else has done, is doing, or will do. Your life task is to do what you can do, and this is totally up to you.

I have a tendency to be competitive. When I feel that I won't do as well as others, I don't get involved. There are so many people out there doing major acts of kindness on a large scale that I feel that what I would do is inferior and therefore not worth doing.

My teacher noticed that I wasn't involved with a group working on a charitable project and asked why. I explained that I didn't feel like doing just a small amount when others were doing so much more.

"You need to limit your focus to what you are doing and ignore what others are doing if that prevents you from doing more yourself," she told me.

It took a lot of effort, but I eventually mastered the ability to limit my focus as she suggested. Now when I do acts of kindness for others, nothing else exists but this person and what I can do for him. This has freed me from comparing what I do with what others do. I am now much more motivated to do what I can and I feel a sense of accomplishment that had always been missing in the past.

FIRST THOUGHTS

W hat are your first thoughts when you meet another person? People who have a strong tendency to be takers, think, "What can this person do for me?" People who have a strong tendency to be critical, think, "What can I find that is negative about this person?" Some people tend to think, "Do I like or respect this person or not?" And others focus on the question, "Do I feel comfortable in the presence of this person?" And yet others think about, "What does this person think of me?"

When you meet someone, let your first thought be, "What can I do for this person?" This way you will view each encounter with a fellow human being as an opportunity to give and help.

It is relatively easy to develop the habit of asking this question. At first, you need to deliberately ask yourself this question over and over again. Asking it enough times will cause it to pop into your mind automatically. After a while, as soon as you meet someone you will hear the question, "What can I do for this person?"

Don't continue to read on right now. Stop for a few minutes, and repeat many times, "What can I do for this person?" Enjoy the process. You can even sing these words with one of your favorite tunes. Feel the joy of elevating yourself.

As you repeat the question, "What can I do for this person?" think of specific people you know. Begin with people you like a lot. Then think of those towards whom you are neutral. Finally think about those with whom you experience difficulty when you deal with them.

We all need the assistance and encouragement of others at one time or another. Even then we can think about how we can help this person whose help we need. We needn't think of this in terms of bartering: He is doing something for me, so I will do something for him. Rather, this can be viewed as part of our general attitude of wanting to help others even more than we want others to help us. Even if someone has more resources than we do, we still might be able to say or do something to enhance his life.

I used to be judgmental towards others. I would automatically focus on, "What is wrong with this person?" and, "What faults can I find?"

I often heard the expression, "When you look for something, you will find it." I readily found the blemishes, the mistakes, the errors, and the limitations. This caused me considerable frustration, anger, resentment, and cynicism. In general, I looked down at others. People felt the negative energy emanating from me, and this created difficulties in my getting along with others.

*What I did was the opposite of what one would do if one want-
ed to win friends and influence people.*

*The turning point came when I was advised to keep asking,
"What can I do for this person?" At first I balked. "Why should I
think of others? Others don't think about what they can do for
me."*

*"What do you have to lose?" I was challenged. "Your present
situation is highly distressful. It makes sense to do all you can
to improve things. Try it for a couple of weeks."*

*So I joined the ranks of those who ask, "What can I do for
this person?" In the beginning, I heard a cynical inner voice,
"Who are you trying to fool? This isn't you."*

*But I was committed to try for at least two weeks and I
intended to keep my word. In just a few days, I experienced a
major shift in the way I felt towards others. It was unbelievable
how powerful this was in changing the way others viewed and
treated me. Much of the constant stress that I formerly felt melt-
ed away. I had more energy than I ever did before, as well as
increased joy. I highly recommend this practice for others. And
that is what I can do for you.*

ENTER THE WORLD OF THE OTHER PERSON

I have a complex personality and rarely feel understood. When I have a difficult issue to deal with, most people I speak to verbally shoot from the hip. They say things that might fit the inner world of others, but not mine. I remember how great it felt to meet someone who didn't offer any advice or suggestions until he understood the entire picture from my perspective. He took my unique personality into consideration before making any helpful comments. And that is why what he told me was so constructive.

I am very emotional. My emotions are intense and don't change as easily as those of most other people I know. When other people tell me, "Just cheer up," or, "Just calm down," it's not a bit helpful.

When you wish to help people, enter their world. To be truly helpful you need to take into consideration: life history, total present situation, unique personality, patterns of emotions, and individualized perceptions and evaluations.

When you enter someone's world, that person no longer feels lonely. You are more likely to avoid making distressful or counterproductive comments. And what you do say could be precisely what this person needs to hear.

Learning to enter the world of another person is a learnable skill. The more people you interview and listen to carefully, the more your expertise will grow.

Probe with sensitivity. Some people would prefer that you don't ask personal questions. But those who wish to be understood will greatly appreciate your probing questions as intending to be helpful and not as prying into their private lives. Here your motivation is very important. If you are asking questions just because of your own curiosity, the person might be offended and protect his privacy. But when your questions are solely for the other person's benefit, they are likely to be appreciated.

Listen to understand. Listen nonjudgmentally. Comprehend why this person did what he did from his perspective. Then your advice and suggestions will be more readily accepted. Your concern for the total welfare of this person will come through and will be appreciated.

BE KIND UNCONDITIONALLY

Once you have done an act of kindness for another person, be grateful if the person is grateful. But don't expect gratitude. Many people lack the ability to express gratitude. If you do your acts of kindness because you hope you will receive gratitude, you are setting yourself up for disappointment.

Some people are very hurt and feel resentful if they help another person and he isn't grateful. When you do an act of kindness, do it wholeheartedly. Do it even if that person will never do anything at all for you. Do kindness unconditionally and you will never regret the good you have done.

"True kindness" is the kindness you do for someone who is deceased. Attending his funeral and being involved in honoring him after his death is the truest level of kindness. Why? Because he will never do anything for you. He can't even say, "Thank you," regardless of how difficult it was for you to attend his funeral. Since you are doing an act of respect which will not be reciprocated by this person, your act of kindness is more elevated.

I used to have many angry quarrels. I would go out of my way to do many things for others, but I didn't feel I was receiving enough gratitude. This would make me angry, and I would rebuke and censure relatives and friends for not being more grateful.

I spoke to someone who advised me, "Take pleasure in the good you do. Let the knowledge that you are doing kind acts be its own reward."

"This sounds too lofty for me," I argued. "I'm a regular human being and it bothers me when my efforts are not met with gratitude."

"Forget about high spiritual levels right now," he said. "Do this out of intelligent self-interest. When you demand the gratitude you don't spontaneously receive, you end up quarreling and everyone loses. By not demanding gratitude, you will end up with more gratitude than before. Please do me a favor and try it out."

He was right. It worked. When others saw that my kindness came from sincere caring and not as a means of obtaining gratitude, the actual gratitude increased immensely. But since I was sincerely prepared to forgo gratitude, I could only win and there was no way to lose.

Whenever I did something for someone, what was uppermost in my mind was, "I hope this person will do something for me in return. If he won't, I should be doing this for someone who will."

This attitude caused me much resentment. A friend of mine consistently did acts of kindness for people who weren't likely to reciprocate. He told me, "When someone does something for another person with the hope that they will do something in return, he is never certain if he will get what he wants. When I joyfully do a kind act unconditionally, I am 100 percent guaranteed to benefit from what I do. It makes sense to get a guarantee on one's investment in time and energy."

II

ONCE YOU GIVE IT AWAY ...

I t has been said with regard to sharing what you have and know with others: Once you give it away, then it's really yours, for you have the eternal merit of the kind act. The money you give to others is no longer material, it has been transformed into spirituality. The ancient alchemists wanted to turn simple metal into gold. That is what you are doing when you share your money with someone in need.

The vital knowledge you share with others truly belongs to you when you pass it on from the data bank in your brain to the brain of another human being. This knowledge will live on and on. That person will transfer it to the brains of others and they will utilize that knowledge themselves and keep passing it on. Your merit keeps growing with the positive effects that mushroom endlessly.

A miser tries to hoard his money. But he is failing to utilize what he owns. If he were to realize how he is limiting his true wealth, he would hasten to find some worthy person, institution, or cause that would benefit from a portion of his fortune. The part that he gives away might seem to diminish the size of his fortune. In reality what he gives away remains his eternal possession and the true size of his fortune is calculated by what he gives and not by what he keeps. Some people use the expression, "He is worth 'X' amount of money." They usually refer to a person's money, investments, and property that has not yet been given away. The expression would be more accurate if the calculations only included what one has donated to others.

The Talmud (*Bava Metzia* 38a) teaches that a person has more pleasure from one share of his own than from nine shares that come from someone else. The money you give, the possessions you lend, and the knowledge you share are what belong to you. This has infinitely more value than what you don't give, lend, or share.

A person may overcome a phobia, a limitation, or a bad habit. That is a praiseworthy achievement. But a greater achievement is when that person shares his knowledge and experiences with others who have similar phobias, limitations, and habits. They are helped with his knowledge. They too can pass this on to others and thus more and more will benefit from the original sharing. The value of the information that was given away expands and expands. If it were to have just remained in the first person's brain cells, it would have eventually disappeared without accomplishing a fraction of what it accomplished by being passed along.

When you have a dilemma — Should I share what I have with others or should I keep it for and to myself? — make the wise decision. Focus on the future outcome of each choice. Give, lend, and share with those who could benefit. And then what is truly yours is increased.

When I was a young child, I resented the idea of sharing my belongings with others. "My toys are mine," I would say. "If I let others use them, then I am losing out. If I share the candies that are mine with others, then I have less."

I retained this attitude as I grew older. I was often too embarrassed to refuse to give and share when I was asked to do so. But I would never volunteer, and I looked for ways and means to hold on to what was mine.

I read somewhere, "Only what you give to others is really yours." This struck a true chord within me. When I kept things, I didn't feel a sense of loss, but I didn't feel expansively wealthy either. I started enjoying giving to others. It was unbelievable how my sense of personal wealth grew as I gave.

ANONYMOUS KINDNESS

There is a very valuable consciousness-raising practice of doing daily acts of kindness without letting anyone know who did them.

There is an incentive to doing acts of kindness when the person for whom you do something knows what you did and is grateful. The expressions of gratitude are a form of bartering. Your kind act is still a kind act, but there are aspects of a business transaction. When others are aware of the kind act you did, there is a sense of obtaining honor and respect. Again this is a form of bartering. But when no one knows what you did, there is a purity and wholeness to your kind act.

At times we might do kind acts because it is difficult for us to refuse. We feel emotionally coerced into doing them. But an anonymous kind act is motivated by a true desire to do acts of kindness.

Enjoying the process of doing kind acts anonymously increases your love for acts of kindness. It enhances your motivation for situations when your kindness is known and appreciated.

But what if I can't find a kind act to do? Major kind acts aren't always available. Somehow you will always be able to find minor kind acts. Just thinking about this every day will have a strong effect on your character.

Some kind acts that people can do anonymously:

- When you are happy with the services provided by an employee, call up his employer and tell him about it.
- When someone starts a new business, tell people you know to patronize that business.
- If you know that someone needs a job, tell a potential employer in his field to contact him.
- Put money in a parking meter when the time left is running out.
- If your friend is hurt about not receiving an invitation to a wedding or another occasion, call up the host to correct this oversight.
- Send an unsigned card saying, "We think that you are great and we wish you well."
- If drinks or food are being served in a big crowd, remind a waiter to serve those sitting at the side.
- Send a helpful book as a gift.
- Send flowers with a note: This is a token of appreciation from someone who respects you.
- Send someone a paid-for ticket to a lecture or course from which he will benefit.
- Send a tape or CD of relaxing music.
- Pay someone's bill (such as a grocery bill) without their knowing who paid it.

- Send a gift subscription for a magazine with a note: This has been paid for by a friend.
- Suggest to others that they praise or compliment someone who could use it.
- Pay a highway toll for the person behind you.
- Send money to someone who is experiencing financial difficulties, and include this note: Some time in the future you will be able to repay this by doing the same for someone else.
- Tell people to do acts of kindness anonymously. The kindness they will do in the future is part of your anonymous kindness.

I was the recipient of an anonymous kindness and I know how much I appreciated it. Someone paid for a month worth of taxis to help me save time. Not knowing who the person was gave me the great feeling that there is someone out there who wants to help me. Not knowing who it was increased its pleasure for me. It made me realize that there are people who truly care about me.

13

"IT'S REALLY NOTHING"

S ome people will be reluctant to accept your help. They hate to bother you or anyone else. They need your reassurance that what you did for them was "really nothing."

When dealing with them you need to minimize your bother factor, even if you had to go out of your way and it took you much time and effort. You might feel a need to let them know how difficult it was and that you were still happy to do it for them. But this will just make them even more reluctant to allow you to help them in the future.

Be careful not to feel resentful if the person you tell, "It was really nothing," believes you. Some people tend to say this, but deep down hope that the person they helped will realize that what they did was a product of much effort. If you want someone to realize that you care about them and therefore were willing to help them at the price of great sacrifice on your part, tell it to them. But do so in a way that conveys the message, "I feel so much joy in helping you that no matter what I do it becomes relatively easy since you are so important to me."

You might want to give someone money because he is presently experiencing great financial difficulties, but that person is the type who doesn't want to take from others. Then creatively find some subterfuge to use to get him the money he needs. Of course, people often see through these ruses, so use one that seems real.

Some examples:

- Tell him that you have some extra money right now that you aren't going to be using. You don't want to leave it in the house and you have reasons why you don't want it to be put into a bank. Could he please do you a favor and hold it for you. You give him permission to spend it on himself now, and he can replace it any time in the future that he finds convenient.
- Buy something from him that you might not really need, and buy it for a higher price than it is available for elsewhere, or for more than it's really worth. This could be an item like a picture he has, an antique that most people wouldn't buy, or some other item that he might not have thought of selling.
- Have a friend give him a used computer or another expensive item. Then have someone else "buy" it from him. Thus he ends up with the money that you wanted him to have, but it was given in a way that did not make him feel uncomfortable.
- Give his employer money to supplement a raise in salary or a bonus.

I was frequently surprised that so many people refused to allow me to help them. Finally, I spoke to a person who constantly did things for other people. "Why do people keep insisting that they don't need my help when I know they really do?" I asked him.

"Can I tell you the truth?" he asked me.

"Of course," I said. "I really want to know even if it's not what I would hope to hear."

"You make it seem like it's extremely difficult for you to do the favors for them. It's in your tone of voice and the expression on your face. Create an inner positive feeling towards helping others and express this verbally and nonverbally."

I was grateful for this painful awareness. I accepted what he said and made the necessary changes. It's unbelievable how people who used to decline my offer of help are now totally open and grateful.

14

LEARN FROM EVERY KIND PERSON YOU MEET

"What has made you such a kind and giving person?" a major philanthropist was asked.

"I learned giving from my father. He wasn't wealthy, yet helping other people financially gave him more enjoyment than spending money on himself."

"How did you develop such a kind personality?" a devotee of service to others was asked.

"I read the biographies of kind people and said to myself, 'This is the way I want to be.'"

"Why do you always invite guests to your home for meals?"

"I was once a stranger in a large city. Being invited to the homes of a few families taught me the value of this hospitality."

Each of us is different. Therefore we can all learn from others. Every person you encounter, infrequently or on a daily basis, has some manner, some patterns, some habits, some attributes from which you can learn. By modeling the strengths and positive qualities of as many people as you can, you develop yourself in ways that you could not do on your own.

By mirroring or modeling another person, you can plug into his positive patterns, states, and qualities. But if you mirror or model might you not also plug into his negative patterns, states, and qualities? Yes, you might. Therefore when you mirror and model do so wisely. Think of the patterns that will make the most positive differences in your life and find appropriate role models. This applies to all areas of your life, especially when it comes to upgrading your level of being kind to other people.

First of all, take note of all those kind, sensitive, and helpful actions that people do for you. Remember what people have done for you already in the past. Try emulating those actions and continue practicing them again and again. Remember the kind words that others have said to you and pass them on to others.

Next, observe the kind words and actions that people say to others. Be on the lookout for kind actions that you witness being done for other people. These patterns can now become yours.

When you read stories about age-old or recent kind acts, you are essentially learning how to become a better person. Look at each story as a source of inspiration and as a practical guide on becoming a kinder person.

Interview people. Ask them, "What have people said to you that has enhanced your life?" and, "What are some things people have done for you?" Each answer is a valuable addition to your mental library.

You never stop learning. No matter how much you think you know, there is always more to learn. Imagine what it would be like to receive a daily report on 100 ways that people on our planet have acted kindly on the previous day. Each day you personally can do something that could be added to that list.

15

HAVE HUMILITY

"I've met some do-gooders who boast and brag so much about the good they do that it makes me sick."

"How dare you speak to me like that. Don't you know that I am a kind person?!"

"I wouldn't be so arrogant as to tell this to others. But in my heart I know that I am great."

Let's face it. We mortals are limited. We have limited knowledge. Limited intelligence. Limited resources, such as money, time, and energy. Let this give you a sense of humility.

No matter how much we do, we probably could have done more and better. So have humility.

Even if we do all that we can, we are only doing our duty. So have humility.

All that you have is a gift from the Creator. Appreciate your gifts. When you realize that it's all a gift, you increase your appreciation for what you have. At the same time this frees you from the arrogance and conceit felt by someone who thinks that he is better than others and that others owe him.

Our goal is to realize that we have an important mission in this world, and that all the good we do is merely part of fulfilling our purpose in life. A truly humble person does not demand honor or recognition for the good that he does.

One of the kindest and most compassionate people I've ever met was also one of the humblest and the most joyous. His face radiated unconditional love and joyous energy.

"How come you are so unassuming," I asked him. "Aren't you proud of what you've already done."

"There is so much more to do," he replied. "I take pleasure in the good I've done. But I realize it's only a drop in the bucket compared to what needs to be done."

"But don't you feel that you are better than others?"

"I focus on what I haven't done yet. This keeps me motivated. Who am I to judge any other human being? When I think of others, I realize my own limitations. I would love to do much more than I am doing. I still experience joy. But how could I possibly feel conceited? I have so much more to do."

16

BEGIN LITTLE BY LITTLE

Some people feel overwhelmed by the concept of consistently doing acts of kindness. "It seems so difficult to keep thinking about others. I have a lot to do for myself and I can't always think of others." The solution is to begin little by little.

You might not have the time and resources to do all that you would really like to do. Be kind with the time and resources you do have. Every small kind act leads to other and greater kind acts.

Every act of kindness makes you a kinder person. Maimonides tells us how to develop a generous personality. Do many small acts of generosity. Instead of giving a single $100 bill to only one person, change the $100 bill into 100 singles. Then give them away one by one. These 100 kind acts are building your character trait of generosity. Just as a building goes up brick by brick, so too you are building yourself act by act.

Each of us finds certain things easier to do than others. What small act of kindness is easiest for you? Keep doing these acts as regularly as possible. "One good deed leads to another," say the Sages (*Ethics of the Fathers* 4:2).

The founder of a major charitable organization with numerous branches began with a few items in his home. He had several vaporizers that he lent out to his neighbors. This grew and grew until the lending of medical equipment free of charge evolved into a national institution of note.

Even if a small act of kindness doesn't lead to major acts of kindness, a small kind act in itself has immense eternal value. Being overwhelmed by thinking too big may prevent you from beginning your journey. Think in terms of one step at a time and you can never tell how far you will eventually go.

I met someone who told me that his life mission is to get people who never do things for others to begin to do so.

"This seems like a difficult task. Why did you choose this as your mission?" I asked him.

"I wish to have as broad an influence as possible. My experience is that once I get a person started on doing acts of kindness, the experience leads to many more kind acts. Getting someone started can be difficult. But once I motivate him to begin, he will eventually be motivated on his own to do much good."

17.

THIS PERSON NEEDS TO BE HELPED VERSUS I NEED TO HELP

There are many people of whom this is true: "I love to help people. But I need to be honest about it. When I want to help someone, I resent other people doing the job that I wish to do. I want to have people as my guests and I don't like it if they cancel out to go elsewhere. When I want to do someone a favor, I dislike it if someone else does it for them. If someone frequently comes to me for advice, I resent it if they go to others instead of me."

When someone is in need of help, the ideal is to want this person to be helped. It is irrelevant who will be the one to effect this. Whether you will be the messenger to help this person or someone else will be chosen, shouldn't make such a difference to you.

People who aren't interested in helping other people don't have this problem. They hope others will help people instead of them. They feel relieved not to be asked. If they are asked and then someone else resolves the issue, they are happy about it. But those who love to help people are disappointed when others do what they wished to do.

When your desire to help others comes from sincerely caring about the other person's welfare, you will feel good about this person's needs being met. You are ready to volunteer to help out, but only because your help is actually needed. When it isn't, seek other outlets for your desire to do acts of kindness.

For many years, I would consult with a wise and compassionate teacher. She would give me advice and encouragement and I benefited greatly from her. Once there was a major decision I had to make and it was more convenient for me to consult someone else. I felt a need to be totally honest with my teacher and I apologized to her for not consulting with her.

"You have no need to apologize," she said with total sincerity. "When you need me, I hope to always be there for you. But you should consult the person you feel is best for you at a given moment. Never feel obligated to ask me for my opinion if you feel that it will be better for you to consult someone else."

I felt relieved that she wasn't upset and both my respect and my gratitude increased greatly.

18

DO MORE THAN ASKED

There are people who prefer to do favors for others when they volunteer to do so. When they are asked, they often consider it a burden. The benefit of being asked by another person is that then you know for certain what this person's needs actually are. Show that fulfilling this person's request is something that you really want to do. How? By doing more than you have been asked to do.

At times we might do what we have been asked to do because we find it difficult to say no. We know that we should do acts of kindness and therefore we do things out of embarrassment. But our going beyond the specifics of what was asked of us is an expression that our true inner will is to do acts of kindness.

Many people hesitate to ask for favors because they don't like to be a burden to others. They don't want others to do things for them just because those people would feel guilty about refusing. When you do more than you have been asked, you demonstrate your sincere willingness to help. We go the extra mile when we enjoy what we are doing or we feel that this is the right thing to do. Doing more than you have been asked will enable the recipient of your kindness to feel better about all that you have done for him before, are doing now, and will do for him in the future. The extra thing you do could be a relatively minor thing, but the benefits are major.

- *I asked him to lend me $500. I was overwhelmed when on his own he offered $2,000, and he told me, "Thank you for asking. It's my pleasure."*
- *I asked my friends if I could stay at their home for a few days. They told me their house was available for even a month. The entire week I was their guest I felt totally at home.*
- *I asked my neighbor if she could watch my children for a couple of hours so I could rest. My neighbor offered to have them stay overnight so I could get a good night's sleep. I felt grateful beyond words.*
- *I asked a few questions about how to use my new computer. I was treated to a full three-hour lesson.*
- *I asked for a lift and expected to walk from my neighbor's house to my own. Instead, the driver went out of his way to take me all the way home.*

19.

DON'T DO UNTO OTHERS

The number one principle for knowing what not to do to others was stated in the Talmud (*Shabbos* 31a) by the sage Hillel: "What you yourself dislike, don't do to another. This is the entire Torah. The rest is commentary."

When we want to say something to another person and aren't certain if we should say it, we can ask ourselves, "Would I want someone to say something similar to me?"

When we have an ethical question about whether a certain business practice would be acceptable, we can ask ourselves, "How would I feel if someone did this to me?"

If someone wants to play a practical joke on another person, he can ask himself, "Would I prefer that someone else not do something similar to me?"

We are different from any other person on the planet. Even if we wouldn't mind if someone said something to us, we should still not say that to someone who might be hurt or offended by those words. It could be that we would find a certain practical joke humorous even though we were the "victim." We nevertheless have no right to cause someone else distress because it wouldn't have bothered us. Hillel's rule is not a license to automatically do to others what we wouldn't mind ourselves. Rather it's a general guideline to make us more sensitive to the potential distress and pain of others.

Build up your awareness of what you would not want others to do to you. Every time someone says or does anything that you find distressful, immediately add it to your mental data base of what you are now totally committed not to do to others. Similarly, if you observe or hear about something that is done to another person and you feel, "I wouldn't like anyone to do that to me," add it to your "I won't do this to others" list.

I asked people to become more aware of what they didn't like others to do to them. Here are some of the results:

- *I used to keep people waiting. Then I noticed how annoyed I became when others made me wait. This motivated me to be more prompt.*
- *I became impatient when people asked questions that I thought they should know on their own. Then someone responded rudely to a question I asked. From then on I made a special effort to be more respectful to others who asked me questions.*
- *I am curious and tend to ask a lot of personal questions. I encountered someone who asked me questions that I wouldn't think of asking others. This gave me a greater awareness that I should carefully weigh what I ask in order not to offend anyone.*

- *When guests came to my home, I would insist that they eat. I was at someone else's home and didn't have an appetite. They kept repeating, "Please eat something. " I said that I wasn't hungry, but they were persistent. I now say, "Perhaps you would like something to eat." But when I get a negative response I don't persist.*
- *I used to tap my fingers on the table. After thinking about Hillel's principle, I noticed that it annoyed me when others tapped on the table. I made a strong resolution to stop and I no longer have this habit.*

20

FORGIVE

At times the greatest kindness you can do for someone is to forgive. Some people will ask you for forgiveness. Others will lack the awareness or courage or humility to ask your forgiveness. Forgive even if you aren't asked to do so. This can be extremely difficult. And that is why it is so elevating.

When we forgive others, we are forgiven. This consciousness will make it easier to forgive. When we forgive others, we let go of the resentment and anger that is so dangerous to our physical and spiritual well-being.

The realization that anyone who comes to us to ask forgiveness is actually a messenger from our loving Creator and powerful King makes it easier to forgive. Our mind is too precious to be filled with thoughts and feelings of hatred and animosity. A mind full of compassion and kindness finds it easy to forgive, and this is the type of thinking that elevates and uplifts.

I used to find it difficult to forgive others if they wronged me. Then one day I unintentionally said something that offend-

ed a person who was mentally unbalanced. After that, every time I met that person he would repeat quite loudly, "I don't forgive you." I asked him to forgive me, but he would refuse.

"You're not really sorry," he would say.

"This is ridiculous," I said to myself. "Why is he holding onto resentment for so long?"

Then I realized that I am guilty of the same thing. Of course, what I am angry about is more serious that what this person is angry about. And I am more subtle in my approach to not forgiving. But what I habitually did was — at the core — just as out of line as what this person did. I committed myself to have a broader perspective and to forgive.

I met a person who told me that a turning point in his life occurred when a homeowner caught him trying to steal valuables. He begged the homeowner not to call the police. The owner looked him straight in the eye and said, "I will forgive you and let you go, but on one condition. I need you to promise me that you will never do this again. I am not naïve to think that everyone who makes this promise will keep it. But I think that you will."

I felt tremendously grateful to him, and said, "I promise."

The man told me to come back for weekly meetings and volunteered to help me straighten out my life. His forgiveness totally transformed the entire course of my life.

I spoke against someone and then deeply regretted it. I went to ask his forgiveness. This was exceedingly difficult for me since I felt embarrassed.

"I understand how tempting it can be to speak against others," he said to me. "I forgive you." I appreciated his kind way of saying this to me and resolved to be much more careful not to speak against others in the future.

21

EVEN IF YOU DON'T FEEL KIND

"This whole idea of considering myself a kind person is for-eign to me. At best, I'll help people once in a while. At worst, I want to be left alone. I can't be bothered by people making demands on me. I would feel as if I were acting if I did kind deeds when I didn't really feel like doing them."

A valuable rule is: "Even if you don't feel like a kind person, you can still act like one."

"But isn't it better to feel kind before you act kind?" is a common question.

It's definitely preferable for our feelings and actions to be in sync with each other and for both to be elevated. Then we are at our best. But the question that needs to be addressed is: "If I don't feel kind, should I congruently not do anything for anyone, or should I incongruently help other people?"

Ask a person who needs a loan, "If someone doesn't feel like lending you money but agrees to do it because it's the right thing to do, would you prefer that the person congruently refuses you, or would you prefer that he lend you the money because he wants to do what is right?"

Or, imagine collapsing while walking down a busy street. Would you prefer that everyone just left you there because they congruently didn't want to spend their time calling an ambulance or trying to revive you? Or, would you prefer that they incongruently did all they could to save your life?

Why should others have to suffer just because you haven't yet integrated the ideals and values that you want to follow and apply?

Those who have internalized a kindness-consciousness are fortunate. They both act and feel in ways that enhance their life and the lives of others. But those who don't yet feel kind will make this feeling their reality by repeatedly doing kind acts. Every kind act you do strengthens your sense of being a kind person.

I am the last person who would have thought that I would ever consider myself a kind person. I am grateful to the one who said to me, "Act and the feelings will come." For me this advice worked and I encourage others to do the same.

22.

THE THRILL OF VICTORY

There are many levels of joy, ecstasy, and euphoria when it comes to the thrill of victory. The degree of the joy will depend on the type of victory and how much it means to the individual who experiences it. Most major victories happen rarely, often once in a lifetime. Throughout the world these often take the form of inter-city and international sports events. The joy of an upset victory in a World Cup, World Series, or Superbowl — for players as well as fans — is very intense. But with these events, the vast majority of people around the world either don't care or were rooting for a team that didn't make it.

Wouldn't it be absolutely wonderful if you could have the thrill of a victory every single day? You can. How? By celebrating the victory of doing a major act of kindness that is difficult. The greater the difficulty, the greater the potential for the joy of victory.

Think of some people for whom you could do something beneficial, but find it difficult to do so. You might feel resentful towards them for one reason or another. You might feel envious. You might feel that they don't do anything or enough for you. Whatever the reason, you find it difficult to do things for them.

Now visualize yourself doing a kind act for one of those people. See yourself going out of your way to help them in ways that make a significant difference in their lives. As you see yourself doing this, imagine a huge stadium full of people cheering for your victory. See and hear and feel the exuberant excitement and enthusiasm of 100,000 ecstatic fans. Or you can imagine a million people cheering for you in a parade down New York's Fifth Avenue. Mentally repeat this over and over again. As you do, you will feel a great sense of victory as you contemplate how you will help the people you find difficult to help.

A variation of this is to imagine yourself doing something that would constitute a glorious and intense triumph. This can involve any area in which you personally would feel euphoric excitement for such a splendid victory. Visualize this vividly until you actually feel the joy of that success. Studies have shown that our hormonal system has actual biochemical responses even though the victory is totally a figment of our imagination. Then see yourself doing a difficult act of kindness. The act might seem relatively small. But if it's difficult for you, it's a victory and worthy of celebration.

When you act externally with enthusiasm and excitement, your inner emotional state mirrors your external patterns. So when you do acts of kindness that are difficult, act externally with the joy of a great victory. As you keep this up, the difficulties will not only be easier, they will be a source of great joy in your life.

Right now think of three acts of kindness you could do that would constitute a victory. Make a commitment to do them. Put it in writing. As you feel the thrill of victory, you will be motivated to continue doing more of these kind acts.

I was living a rather boring existence. I shared my feelings with someone who was much more excited about life than I was. We compared notes and I saw that the general condition of our lives wasn't that different.

"What is it about your life that gives you so much excitement?" I asked him.

"I have the excitement of victories every single day," he told me.

"How do you manage that?" I asked.

"Each day I think of an act of kindness that would be difficult for me to do and I follow through," he replied. "This creates daily excitement for me. If more people realized how wonderul their lives would be if they practiced this, we would live in a happier world. These are non-competitive victories where everyone involved is a winner."

23

BETTER TO TRY AND FAIL THAN NOT TO ATTEMPT AT ALL

When we feel certain that we will succeed, we feel motivated to take action. When we feel absolutely certain that we can do nothing about a situation, we don't try. Why try to do something that is impossible? The challenge is to take action when we aren't certain whether or not we will succeed.

Some people hesitate to take action because they are afraid that they might fail. And if they fail, they might view themselves as failures. Not what our egos want!

But when you try to help someone and sincerely do what you can, you are successful even if what you try to do does not work out the way you would have wished. The act of trying is a magnificent accomplishment.

When someone sees that you are trying to help him, he feels pleasure that there is someone who cares enough about him to try. He is not alone. He has you.

You might think that your efforts have not been fruitful, but you can never know. You might try to encourage someone to believe in himself and his strengths. He fights you tooth and nail. He raises every argument in the book explaining why he can't believe in himself. He defends his right to a lack of self-esteem and a low self-image. What you say to him might seem to go in one ear and right out the other one. But the reality is that what you say may remain dormant for a long time. Then one day, presto! Your words hit home. He recalls your belief in him and he begins to believe in himself. The only way to guarantee failure is to refrain from trying. When you do make an effort to be kind, your kind words and actions might set off a chain reaction. You lift this person a tiny bit. And now he has the energy to go much further than you would have believed.

A doctor pronounced an unconscious patient dead. A devoted friend of that person refused to give up. He had someone work on artificial respiration until an ambulance arrived to take the person to a hospital. At the same time, he asked all those nearby to pray for the recovery of this person. When the patient made a seemingly miraculous recovery, the doctor stated that this experience had given him the total resolve to keep on trying in the future beyond what he had been doing until that point.

The learning-disabled student had given up on ever being a scholar. So had most of his teachers. One even said, "Your chance of being a scholar is less than the chance of hair growing on the palm of my hand." One compassionate teacher, however, refused to give up. He repeated each idea scores of times. His student flourished to the astonishment of everyone who had tried to teach him before.

A friend suggested that I exercise for my health. He repeated this many times and while I agreed with him, I did nothing about it. Finally, one day I said, "All right. I'll start." I am grateful for this person's persistence in urging me to guard my health. Every repetition was part of the conditioning that eventually had a practical effect.

24

NOTE YOUR DISTRESSFUL EXPERIENCES

When I was in the hospital for complex surgery, it gave me a whole new understanding of what it feels like to be helpless and totally dependent on the good-will of others. I kept thinking, "Now I know what it's like when others talk about being nervous before surgery." I remember my post-surgery distress. I felt grateful for those who spoke to me gently and gave me visions of hope. That was five years ago and since then I have been able to give comfort to others in a similar situation because I have been there myself.

I lost my job at the worst possible time in my life. I was financially and emotionally vulnerable. Fortunately, I became successful. I was able to look back at that experience as the turning point in my life. Not only did that lay the foundation for my financial success, it also made me much more sensitive to what others go through when they lose their jobs. I utilized what I learned from the experience to give encouragement and advice to many others throughout the years.

When I am alert and full of flowing energy, my mind works quickly. I am immediately able to understand what I read and hear. Even when I don't understand something, I know that with patience I eventually will. But when I am tired or in an unresourceful state, I feel overwhelmed. I can't understand even simple ideas. I can look at a page and it just doesn't register. I forget what I hear in just a few seconds. This pattern has enabled me to be sensitive to those who experience this response in particular areas and all the more so to those who experience this all the time.

I went through a bout of depression. It didn't last very long. But I couldn't shake it as quickly as I would have wished. From then on I stopped offering simple platitudes to others who were depressed.

Every difficulty in your life builds up your mental library of what it's like to go through hard times. Every mistake enables you to empathize with others who make mistakes. Every time you become frustrated or angry, you gain a better understanding of others who feel this way. Make note of all your worries and your fears. Make note of your uncomfortable or embarrassing moments. These — together with every injury, illness, and wound — help you to become more sensitive to the suffering of others.

Make note of what you didn't appreciate hearing from others when you were suffering. And remember the comments and suggestions of others that you did appreciate. What did they say?

How did they say it? Keep in mind that every individual is unique. You might have gained from what someone said to you, but someone else would not find that beneficial. The responses you liked can serve as a starting point when comforting others.

When you view your own pain, distress, and suffering as tools for empathy and understanding, you have a reframe that will elevate every difficult experience throughout your life. You will never suffer just for yourself. You are always learning lessons about how you can help others. Without life experience, a person can be well-meaning and full of good intentions, but might say the wrong things. With experience, you have greater insight. Your intuitions become more accurate. So remember past moments of distress and view them as great resources for helping others. May you never suffer, but since we all suffer to some degree let your own suffering be a source of light, comfort, and healing to others in distress.

25

SHARING YOUR EXPERIENCES

"T he suffering of many, is half a consolation." When someone has a problem or difficulty, it is comforting and consoling to hear from someone, "I, too, had a similar problem."

Those who have experienced a similar situation or occurrence may find that the very way they solved their problem can serve as a solution for the person to whom they are talking. At times a different solution might be needed, but if one person could find a solution, it proves that the problem is solvable. And even if an immediate solution is not forthcoming, hearing from someone that he too experienced what you are experiencing lightens the burden somewhat. Be very careful not to needlessly say anything negative about other people when you share your experiences.

My mother would reprove me, tell me stories and aphorisms, but she would never tell me that she experienced the same things that I did. My mother was the greatest teacher I ever had. But I wish that she would have shared with me some of the difficulties that she experienced. And now that she is gone, I wish that she would have shared with me the feelings she experienced when her mother died.

I visit people who have cancer because I, too, had cancer and recovered fully. I have a vivid memory of speaking to one of the greatest scholars of the generation when I was ill. He unbuttoned his shirt and showed me his long scar. "That scar is 18 years old," he told me. "And I have lived a healthy and productive life since then."

Those words encouraged me tremendously. After I recovered fully myself, I was advised to visit people with similar conditions and give them encouragement. I have been told many times that sharing my story was a source of great encouragement.

I had a rough childhood. Many people who experienced what I did would have given up. I almost did many times. But I persevered and overcame the gravity of my childhood experiences. I share this with as many people as I can in order to give them a vision of what it is possible for them to achieve — even though they had a very difficult start in life.

I am very shy and am easily intimidated by tough people. I am now a sought-after public speaker and can easily speak to groups of any size. When I first began teaching, I found it very difficult to have eye contact with my students. I felt that it was impossible for me to confront anyone. I have come a long way. When I share this with other people who are shy and reserved, I observe their faces light up. "I see that there is hope for me," they often say.

26

EXPRESS GRATITUDE

Even when you are on the receiving end of someone else's kindness, you can do something to increase kindness in the world. Express your gratitude for the kindness rendered to you in a way that will cause the person doing the kindness to have a greater desire to do even more acts of kindness.

It's not worth doing things for others. I went out of my way to help someone and he just mumbled a thank you. He was not a bit grateful. These days people lack gratitude. I'll think twice before I go out of my way for someone else in the future.

People tend to generalize. If someone isn't grateful the only proof there is about a lack of gratitude is that this particular individual lacks this attribute. This is not proof that others also do. Since we tend to generalize — a tendency which is often a vital necessity for dealing with life — one may be less willing to help others if people have not expressed their gratitude in the past. We should do acts of kindness unconditionally. But it is normal for people to want to know that the recipients of their kindnesses are appreciative. Lack of gratitude by one person breeds the attitude, "People aren't grateful."

I did this person a major favor. It was difficult for me to do it. But I felt that it was the right thing to do. I can take it if someone doesn't express gratitude. But all this person expressed was criticism. He had the rudeness to tell me, "Once you do something for someone, do it right. You did six things wrong." He actually pointed out six trivial things that I could have done better. If he had spoken in a grateful tone of voice and was just giving me feedback from which to learn, it wouldn't have been that bad. But he was irritated and his voice and face told me how contemptuous he was of my way of doing things. Next time let him and others like him find another victim. I'm staying away.

If you feel a need to correct something someone did in the course of doing a kindness for you, begin and end with gratitude and praise. Feel and express respect for the person and let this be manifest in your voice and face.

I did a small favor for a person and it was amazing how much he appreciated it. He was so profuse in his praise that you'd think I did something really great. It was easy for me to help him. In the future, I'll be happy to do other things for him and people like him. He made me feel so good about myself. I told him that it was nothing, and he said with a smile, "Every act of kindness is a wonderful thing."

I met someone who clearly loved to do acts of kindness for others. I wanted to learn from him, so I asked, "How did you become such a kind person?"

He modestly replied, "I can't take the credit for it myself. I owe it all to my grandfather. He was elderly and frail. I visited him quite frequently. It was such a pleasure to be in his presence. He had a great smile. The quality I loved most was his explaining how everything I did for him was so helpful and beneficial. When I gave him a glass of water, he would say, 'Thank you so much. I was so thirsty. My mouth was dry and I had visions of becoming dehydrated. Then you were so kind to give me a glass of water. That was so wonderful of you. You saved my life.' I knew he was exaggerating, but he was sincerely grateful. He would give a mini-speech each time I did something for him, telling me how much my actions meant to him. This taught me to see what I was doing for someone from the point of view of the person I was helping. Years later when I think of kindness, I think of my wonderful grandfather and I see his smile. Even if some individuals aren't grateful, I know my grandfather would have appreciated the good I do. This is a powerful motivator for me."

27

TRANSCENDING ULTERIOR MOTIVES

I t is normal to have ulterior motives when you try to help others. The ultimate ideal is to transcend them. Denying them causes you to hold onto them. Acknowledge any ulterior motives you have and then you will be on the road to overcoming them.

The goal is to do acts of kindness out of love for kindness and out of love for people. It means doing kindness for the pure benefit of the people for whom you are doing it. The focus is on helping others and not on what you personally gain. Since we are human, it is natural for us to have ulterior motives at the beginning. Some of them are:

- Doing kindness in order to feel that you are a good person.
- Doing kindness so the recipient will do you favors in return.
- Doing kindness so other people will have greater respect for you.
- Doing kindness in order to save yourself from the embarrassment of what people will think if you refuse.

- Doing kindness so you can boast about it.
- Doing kindness so the recipient will be indebted to you.
- Doing kindness so you will be loved because you are terrified that you might be unlovable.

This does not mean that we should wait to begin to do acts of kindness until we are able to have totally pure motivations. It's impossible to tell how long that will take. It does mean, however, that it is imperative for us to recognize why we are doing what we are doing. It's normal to have mixed emotions. We do a kind act partly because we want to help another person or because we care about him, but also because we want this person to help us or because we want to feel good about ourselves.

When you meet someone who has a sincere love for kindness, you can tell. His entire being conveys this message, "I'm glad you asked me. Whatever I possibly can do for you, it is my great pleasure to do. You don't owe me anything at all for what I have done. And please feel free to ask me again in the future." Such a person lives a joyous life because of the goodness of his heart. This is a goal worth striving for.

"I remember how hurt I was when I was told that my motivation for doing kindness was my wanting to be liked," the young man told me. "I argued that I did kindness for its own sake.

"It was suggested that I think about it for a moment. If I had to choose between helping a person who would be angry

at me for not helping him or helping someone who needed my help even more but wouldn't have any complaints against me for not helping him, whom would I choose to help?

"I had to acknowledge that fear of disapproval would play a decisive role in my choice. This awareness helped me upgrade my motives."

28

"IF I WERE ..."

Questions that begin with, "If I were ...?" can give us a new perspective. Here are some possibilities:

- "If I were this person, what would I want others to do for me?"
- "If I were given a life mission to help this person, what would I do?"
- "If I were this person's best friend, what would I do for him?"
- "If I were at the ultimate level of compassion and kindness, what would I say or do now?"
- "If I were going to be treated by others the way I treat this person, what would I say or do?"

We might not always be able to live up to the standards suggested by these questions. But they give us a different viewpoint from which to see the situation.

If we were this person, what would we be hoping that others would do for us? We view others in need from the outside. Imagining that we were this person enables us to see things from his point of view. If I felt the same need that he feels, what would I hope that others would do for me? If I were in the same predicament or had the same problem, what would I want others to do for me?

We might not consider someone else's needs as important to us. To us this person might be just one of many individuals who have needs, wants, and problems. But if we were to view meeting his needs and solving his problems as our own life task and obligation, what we could do for him increases in priority and importance.

A best friend will go beyond the call of duty to help his buddy. Some things will seem too difficult to do for an acquaintance or even a good friend. But if someone is our best friend, we will make sacrifices that we would not ordinarily be prepared to make.

There exist unlimited levels of kindness and compassion. We are all at different levels along a continuum. A person who has no connection with these attributes probably will not be reading this book. Only the rare human being is on the highest level. Regardless of our present level, when we are prepared to view a situation from the highest level, we will see beyond what we ordinarily would.

If we would be aware that we are deciding our own fate by the way we treat others, we would go out of our way to do all we could. Of course, we can't maintain this level consistently with everyone we encounter who needs our help. But every once in a while, this will do wonders for upgrading our level of kindness.

And one last, "If I were ..." question: "If I were going to view this as my final opportunity to do one last good deed in this world, what would I do?" As you contemplate this question, you will experience its amazing power. Eventually we will all be faced with our actual one last opportunity — and we never know when it will be.

I used to say, "If I were ..." as a way of getting out of helping people. I would say things like:

- *"If I were a rich man I would help people out, but I don't have a lot of money."*
- *"If I were a person with more time, I would do more for others. But I'm always too busy."*
- *"If I were brighter I could help others with my knowledge. But what do I really know?"*

Then I found the power of a more helpful, "If I were ..." statement. "If I were this person what would I want me to do for him?" This opened my eyes to the plight of the people who needed my help. Then I found that I had more resources than I realized.

29

DON'T WAIT FOR AN INVITATION

When it comes to doing acts of kindness for others, don't wait until you are asked. As soon as you recognize a need, volunteer to do something about it. Let your love for kindness be so strong that you cherish each opportunity. Take the initiative to approach people you can help and don't necessarily wait until they approach you. You don't need a formal invitation to ask someone, "What can I do for you?"

- *I knew a person who always had with him numerous items people frequently needed. Items such as pens and pencils, scissors, erasers, rubber bands, paper clips, needle and thread, scotch tape, a small hole puncher, a stapler, envelopes, sheets of paper, stamps, adhesive bandages. When someone needed any of these items he immediately volunteered, "Here, I have some I can give you."*
- *I have a friend who doesn't wait for anyone to ask him for directions. When he sees someone looking at a map, he asks,*

"Can I help you?" If he hears someone asking for directions and the response isn't clear, he approaches the person and tells him step by step how to get to his destination.

- *I remember commenting in passing to someone I hardly knew that I was short of money. He immediately offered to lend me a large sum. I later heard that this was his usual practice. He didn't wait until someone asked him for a loan.*
- *My father would always look for opportunities to give people rides even if they didn't ask him.*
- *When I carry something heavy, I am very grateful to those who ask if they can help me carry it. I prefer not to bother people and ask them unless I absolutely can't manage myself.*
- *An acquaintance of mine approaches new people in town and says, "Hello, I think you are new here. I'm a long-time resident. What would you like to know about our city?"*
- *Whenever my cousin goes shopping, she asks others, "What do you need in the store? I'll be happy to get it for you."*
- *My brother has a cell-phone. When he hears someone say, "I have to make a call. Where is the closest phone?" he offers the use of his cellular phone.*

When someone offers to do an act of kindness for you without your asking, add that to your mental library of what you, too, can do for others without their having to ask you.

30

VIEW WITH COMPASSION

When you watch other people, what you see will depend on what is important to you or what interests you at the time. A barber will notice styles and quality of haircuts. A tailor will notice clothing. A salesman will notice if this person seems like a potential customer. A pickpocket will notice the likelihood of perpetrating and getting away with his crime. A critical person will notice what is wrong with people. And a compassionate person will notice opportunities to be compassionate. Be compassionate. It will elevate you greatly.

Whenever you see someone who is in distress or who is crying, it is a time to be compassionate. Whenever you see someone who is lost, it is a time to be compassionate. Whenever you see someone who needs a loan, it is a time to be compassionate. Whenever you see someone who is angry, it is a time to be compassionate. Whenever you see someone with faulty character traits, it is a time to be compassionate. Every fault or lack or limitation or mistake or need of another person is a wake-up call for you to be compassionate.

When you view someone with compassion, you don't condemn or insult. When you view someone with compassion, you don't ignore his or her needs. When you view someone with compassion, you don't condescend. When you view someone with compassion, you say kind words and do what you can to help. When you view someone with compassion, you yourself become more of a compassionate person.

Isn't there a danger in having too much compassion? Yes, the Talmud (*Pesachim* 113b) states that a person who has an excessive amount of compassion will live a life that's not really living. There is so much suffering in the world that if you view everyone's suffering as your own, it will be impossible to bear such a heavy burden. But when your compassion is balanced and is the appropriate measure for your unique personality, your compassion will enhance your life and the lives of many others.

I witnessed a father berating his young son in a brutal manner. The son was cringing and you could see the terror on his face. I was walking with an older friend and I whispered to him, "I can't just walk by. I have to do something."

"What do you plan to do?" my friend asked me.

"I'm going to tell off that father. The way he speaks makes me furious. No child should be treated like that."

"It's great that you have compassion for that child. And we need to have compassion for the father also. It's obvious that if he treats his son like this, he was treated this way by others. If you just scream at the father, he most likely will take out his frustration and embarrassment on his son later on."

I watched my friend approach the father. With sincere care and concern he said to him, "It's obvious that you care about your child. And it's obvious that your child has done things to get you angry. I also have children and I also lose my temper. Can we please talk? I have some ideas that have helped me. You know your child better than I do. But perhaps my experiences can be helpful for you also."

The tone of voice of my friend was respectful and compassionate. I was amazed to see the father — whom I viewed as a terrible, evil person — calm down right before my eyes.

"I thank you for your offer," the father said. "I feel at a total loss. I hate losing my temper, but I do it over and over again. I would be extremely grateful if you would give me some tips on being a more effective parent."

The power of compassion that I witnessed was unbelievable. The very next time I observed that father interact with his son, I saw a remarkable improvement.

31

THERE, BUT FOR THE CREATOR'S WILL, GO I

I t's easy to view other people's problems and difficulties as their issue. It has nothing to do with us and we would never be in their situation. Who can really tell? No human being can ever know what the future has in store. Scary, isn't it? It is possible that you will never be in the same situation as this person. But that is only because the Creator has not willed for you to be tested and challenged this way.

When you realize that if it were the Creator's will you would have the same life challenges, you will be more empathetic to the plight of those who suffer. You will encounter individuals who are homeless, deformed, or handicapped in various ways. Treat each person the way you would wish to be treated if you were in this person's shoes.

> • *I am a physician. When I treated patients, I looked at them as being in a totally different category than myself. Many considered me arrogant, and I don't blame them. Then I suffered a heart attack and I was a patient in a hospital.*

I experienced what it was like to be totally dependent on the will of others. From then on I saw myself in every patient I treated.

- *I tried an experiment. I dressed in rags and went to a place where no one knew me. I was going to act and feel like a homeless beggar for an entire day. What an experience! From then on I said a kind word to each beggar I passed. I remembered how much I appreciated the kind words people said to me — and I was only doing this as an experiment. Afterwards, I saw myself in every homeless person I encountered.*

- *I was financially well-off. I used to look down at people who, I felt, weren't driven to use their full potential to make money. I viewed them as lazy and unmotivated. Then I suffered a serious financial setback through no fault of my own. I made a comeback and while I had been close to losing all that I had, I was once again well-off financially. This experience gave me a new sensitivity to the plight of the poor. When I was going through my crisis, I was depressed and couldn't think straight. I lacked the energy to do the things I knew I should do. Knowing what it's like to be in a state like that prevents me from being judgmental of others.*

- *I met a brilliant scholar who was unbelievably patient with those who had learning disabilities. When dealing with someone retarded, he was willing to repeat simple ideas over and over again. I asked him how he developed*

*such patience. "My intellect is a gift," he replied. "I was
born with a quick mind. My speed of comprehension and
total recall are gifts that could have been given to others.
Each person has a unique mission in this world. I appreciate what I have been given. But I could have been given
an entirely different brain. Even now, a brain injury or
Alzheimer's would limit my mental functioning. Keeping
these thoughts in mind, I find it relatively easy to be compassionate towards those who have not been given the
same gifts as I have."*

32

LISTEN

Listening to someone is a great act of kindness. It is an act of respect. It might appear to be passive, but being a good listener is a skill that takes effort. Being a great listener is an art, an art that you can learn for the betterment of all those who will appreciate your listening to them with your entire being.

When we listen to someone, it is common for us to interrupt before that person is finished. We are often busy, or distracted, or bored. The skill of listening consists of focusing your total attention on the person to whom you are listening.

Think of a specific time when you were totally fascinated by what someone was telling you. Remember how you leaned forward, how your total attention was on the speaker. You probably had eye contact or focused on the person's mouth as the words flowed forth.

Observe people who are great listeners. Look at their faces. Pay attention to their posture. Listen to the comments they make. Emulate them and you will upgrade the quality of your own listening.

Remember a time when someone was interested in listening to what you had to say. Remember how good it felt. Remember the specific details that indicated to you that you were being listened to.

Those whom others find interesting or fascinating have less of a need for your listening skills. You personally can gain a lot from them and it's highly worthwhile to be a good listener.

The people who will gain the most from your listening are those who are rarely listened to. These are people who suffer and have a strong need to share their feelings with others. They might have a tendency to repeat themselves. Since their talking helps lighten their burden, you are doing an act of kindness by listening. When you are doing someone an important service, your time is being well spent.

When you listen, make brief comments that convey the message that you are paying attention and understand what is being said:

- "I hear."
- "I hear loud and clear."
- "I see."
- "I am getting the picture."
- "That makes sense."
- "That must have been very difficult."
- "That sounds painful."
- "I'm sorry."
- "Wow!"
- "That was really something."
- "Remarkable."
- "Yes, please tell me more."

Think of three people who would especially appreciate your listening to them. Go out of your way to find opportunities to build up your listening skills as you build up your compassion.

I used to feel that being listened to is highly overrated. I was not such an emotional person and felt that people waste too much time talking about how they feel. But then I went through several major crises at the same time. A member of my family had a serious illness. A close friend of mine had suddenly died. I lost my job and had a difficult time finding a new one. The financial pressures kept adding up.

I was traveling on a plane to a job interview. The person I sat next to was intelligent and kind. I began telling him where I was going and why. He listened with his entire being and I felt as I talked to him that he was sharing my burden. I felt lighter as I spoke. At the end of the trip I thanked him profusely for helping me so much. After speaking to him I felt much better than I had in a long time.

"All I did was listen," he said with a smile. I could see that he knew the power of being a good listener. Now I know it also, for the first time.

33

READING BODY LANGUAGE

Our facial expressions and body language convey messages. When we are intensely joyous, enthusiastic, or excited, we convey a very different message than when we are overwhelmed, sad, or angry. When we feel these emotions strongly, the messages can easily be read by anyone who has even a minimal knowledge of how people on planet earth react. However, there are unlimited nuances in the middle that leave considerable room for error or misinterpretation.

Develop an expertise for noticing the facial expressions and body language of those who need help. These external forms of communication serve as announcements that tell us, "I am in distress. Please help me." Notice the look of confusion, fear, sadness, anxiety, and of being lost. Whenever possible, react with the question, "Is there anything I can do to help you?"

Don't take things at face value. Some people don't like to bother others or to feel that they can't do everything on their own. They might say, "Everything is all right." Their facial expression and body language will tell you if everything is really all right or not. Some people will be relieved and grateful if you insist on helping them even though they said they don't need your help. Others will really not want your help. Be respectful of their right not to accept help when you feel that a situation is not one of danger to their well-being. When someone's health is in danger, even if they tell you that they are all right and don't need medical attention, if their demeanor says otherwise, insist on getting them proper health care.

Be aware of your own facial expression and body language when someone asks you for help or assistance. When you are sincerely happy to help someone, your face and tone of voice will give a congruent message when you say, "I'll be happy to help you." If you really are annoyed, your face, tone of voice, or body language will deliver an incongruent message. If you are aware of this, you can use it as feedback from which to learn that you still need to work on increasing your love for doing acts of kindness.

You can be of great help to people by pointing out ways for them to project friendlier and more confident non-verbal messages with their face and posture. One way to do this with one who is open to suggestion is to ask him to describe how he feels when he is joyous, enthusiastic, or confident. Then have him sit, stand, and walk in ways that give off positive messages about his self-image and state. This is especially valuable for a person who has an important interview with someone he has never met before. Have him actually feel the joy or confidence, and then his body language will be an expression of his inner state. If someone finds this difficult to do, then working on facial expressions and body language could be an effective beginning.

I went to the head of personnel in a large organization and told him that I was seeking a job. "Perhaps you have an opening for me?" Instead of making an offer, he told me to speak to that organization's counselor. He didn't tell me why I should speak to him. When I told the counselor that I was told by the C.E.O. to speak to him, he smiled. The way he spoke to me and looked at me conveyed his warmth and concern. He told me that my way of speaking and body language are an expression of lack of confidence and lack of a positive self-image. I replied that I personally felt that my self-image was in order. I totally believed in myself and my abilities.

"Then it's just a matter of changing the way you talk, walk, stand, and sit," he said to me, with total confidence in my ability to improve in these areas relatively quickly.

He mirrored me to show me how I looked and sounded. I hadn't realized how insecure and unconfident I appeared to others. He then modeled the look and sound of confidence. I practiced with him. We went outside and approached complete strangers and spoke to them with confidence. He then introduced me to other members of the organization in a way that made me feel great about myself. I saw that when I modeled him, people reacted to me in a way that reflected my new state of being. I have kept this up over time. It was unbelievable to me how changing my posture, facial expression, and tone of voice effected such a transformation in my own feelings and in other people's perception of me.

34

MAKE IT HAPPEN

A question to ask yourself each day is, "What can I make happen today?"

If you know that someone would appreciate hearing from their cousin, make it happen. " 'X' would greatly appreciate hearing from you. Your call would mean a real lot to him."

If you know that someone is looking for an invitation to another person's home, make it happen. Tell the person how much his invitation would be appreciated.

If you know that someone is looking for a job, do what you can to make it happen.

If someone you know is looking to buy a house, be on the lookout for one that might meet his needs.

At times someone won't think of asking you to help him make something happen. He might not know that you could make it happen for him. He might not want to bother you. And at times he might not be aware of possibilities that would enhance his life. Even if you aren't asked, think of ways to make things happen for people.

What changed my life was that a friend told me about a course that he felt would enable me to develop my dormant talents. He contacted the office of the school and found out details. He even offered to lend me the money to take the course and said that I could pay it back little by little with my earnings. This was exactly what I needed.

I wanted to become a public speaker. I loved speaking but hated the logistics of making the necessary arrangements. Someone who felt people would gain from hearing me told me, "Don't worry about a thing. I'll take care of all the arrangements. All you need to do is show up and share your ideas." That was wonderful of him. It is to his credit that so many have benefited from the lectures.

It took me quite a while to find the person I married. I was apprehensive about getting married. I probably would have been single for many more years if it were not for a friend who sought out a compatible mate for me and persistently did everything possible to make sure things would work out, which they did — fabulously well.

35

PRAYING FOR SOMEONE'S WELFARE

I highly recommend my doctor to others. Not only did he treat me in a way that reflected his sincere caring, he also prayed for me. Following treatment, he wrote down the relevant facts so he would remember to include me in his prayers.

You won't always be able to solve everyone's problems. You can't always figure out the best solution. Your knowledge and resources might not enable you to meet all this person's needs. But you can always pray.

When you pray for the welfare of another person, you are expressing your awareness that true power belongs to the One Above. Your praying for another person is an expression of your feelings of concern and compassion. Every time you pray for someone's welfare, you are becoming a more spiritual person.

Studies have shown that sick people who have people praying for them have a better and quicker rate of recuperation. Rabbi Noah Weinberg frequently asks people — even those who seem far from being religious — "Were your prayers ever answered?" And most people reply that they have been.

When you pray, you connect with the Creator and Sustainer of the universe. This expands your entire consciousness. As you pray for another person, you greatly elevate yourself.

- When you hear that someone is ill or injured, pray for his recovery.
- When someone starts a new business or job, pray for his success.
- Whenever people tell you about their problems or troubles, pray that they find a solution.
- When a couple gets married, pray that their marriage will be successful.
- And pray that you will successfully be able to help many people throughout your life.

I had a serious illness. Fortunately I had an almost miraculous recovery. What helped me the entire time was the knowledge that so many people were praying for me. A few friends contacted as many people as they could — both in person and through e-mail — and asked them to pray for me. I kept getting feedback that many hundreds of people were praying for my health. It had an amazing effect on my emotional state throughout the entire experience. I am grateful to each and every one of those individuals.

36

BLESS PEOPLE IN YOUR MIND

I know an individual who excelled in the ability to make people fell good about themselves. "What thoughts go through your mind when you meet someone new?" I asked him.

"I always mentally bless people with success in what is important to them," was the reply.

When you wish people success in your mind, you radiate positive energy. Even though others don't know exactly what you are thinking, they pick up positive energy. As King Solomon wrote (*Proverbs* 27:19), "As water reflects a face back to a face, so one's heart is reflected back to him by another." When your heart and mind generate positive energy, others feel good about themselves and good about you.

All too many people think critical or negative thoughts about others. This is noticeable in the look in their eyes and in their facial expression. With very critical people, the victims can feel quite uncomfortable. How can these people change? They can begin by seeing the good in others and blessing them in their minds.

Bless people in your mind whether they are people you know or people you are seeing for the first time, whether they are people you especially like or you don't, for whatever reason.

Whenever you see that someone has a troubled, worried, or sad look on his face, bless him in your mind. Wish him healing. Wish him solutions. Wish him joy.

Some of the thoughts you can think are:

- "I wish this person much happiness."
- "I wish this couple marital harmony and unity."
- "I wish this person financial success."
- (Upon seeing a person who is angry:) "I wish this person inner peace."
- "I wish this person a healthy child."
- "I wish this student success in his studies."

When one's mind is full of blessings for others, the very first to benefit from those blessings is the one radiating those good wishes.

An intuitive person with a sharp eye who used to be super critical shared with me, "I used to view people negatively. If someone had a fault, that's all I saw. And who doesn't have faults. I projected a subtle message to people that they were unworthy and of less value than myself. I would get feedback that people tended to feel uncomfortable in my presence.

"Long ago a friend told me, 'Bless people in your mind.' This went in one ear and out the other. But recently I heard someone say it again. For some reason I was more receptive to it. I

can attest that this is a powerful practice. I now recommend this to everyone I can. Again and again I hear from people that they enjoy my company. I had never heard this before I started mentally blessing people."

37.

HELP THE SAME PERSON OVER AND OVER AGAIN

$\int$ ome people need your help only once in a while. Others will need your help over and over again. Each act of kindness is a separate entity of immense value. If you do 100 acts of kindness, they are 100 sources of light whether they were done to a hundred different people or to the same person.

I kept asking the same person to lend me money. I always paid back within a few days. I felt apprehensive about asking him again and again. After a while, I would apologize profusely, "I'm sorry for bothering you so often."

"It's not a bother," he replied. "If someone owns a business, he makes the same profit whether the old customers keep buying from him or if each day there are new customers. I'm glad to be able to lend you money whenever you need it. It's a source of pleasure for me and I don't consider it a bother at all. Please keep coming back to borrow whenever you need to. You don't

have to look for a new person to ask. On the contrary, your asking me is a sign that you believe in my wanting to help you and I consider this a compliment and vote of confidence."

I was immensely relieved by his attitude. I realized that I would have gotten annoyed if the same person had bothered me again and again. This encounter taught me to be grateful to those who give me opportunities to become a kinder person.

I was depressed and going through a long period of stressful situations. I needed to call people for encouragement and strength. When I called on the phone, I could tell if they were thinking, "Oh no, not another time." When someone sounded sincerely happy to help me even though I had called numerous times, I was extremely grateful. It was these good-hearted souls who saved my life.

I had a close relative who was suffering from Alzheimer's disease. He would ask questions and forget the answers a few minutes later. I was finding it difficult to answer the same questions over and over again.

I recalled an idea I had heard from Rabbi Chaim Shmulevitz, the late Rosh HaYeshivah of the Mirrer Yeshivah. The Talmud (Eruvin 54b) describes how Rabbi Praida would repeat each idea to a slow student 400 times. Once the student was distracted by someone who came to extend an invitation to Rabbi Praida. Rabbi Praida said that he would go after he finished teaching his student. After the usual 400 reviews,

Rabbi Praida asked his student if he understood that day's lesson. The student said that the thought of his teacher's imminent departure greatly distracted him and he couldn't concentrate as well as he usually did.

"Don't worry," Rabbi Praida replied. "I'll repeat the idea even another 400 times."

Why did this great teacher spend so much time with this limited student? Rabbi Chaim Shmulevitz explained that the teacher improved in the attribute of patience each and every time he repeated an idea. These were 400 exercises to integrate the trait of patience.

This influenced me to become more patient with my relative, both for his sake and my own. I felt good each time I repeated something. What was most amazing to me was the fact that I could now enjoy something that was previously a source of irritation. I hope to be able to apply this reframe in many areas of my life.

38

THE WAY YOU SEE PEOPLE

I see people as selfish, self-centered, defensive, and incompetent. And I've seen this proven again and again. If people were better, I would be able to treat them better.

I see people as distant and unfriendly. This causes me to close up. And they probably see me the same way, even though inwardly I see myself as a friendly person.

I see people as open, warm, and kind. Whenever they aren't this way, it's because at this moment they're not really themselves. I've seen so many people open up and reveal that they are warm and kind that I know this is the reality of the human condition.

The way you see people is the way they will be in your presence. You the observer have a major effect on the person with whom you interact. Radiate positive energy and this positive energy will be reflected back to you again and again.

People who view others with negative lenses bring out the worst in others. People who are fearful of others and are easily intimidated, fail to bring out the best. And those who view others in a positive light without being naïve or blinded by wishful thinking will elicit the goodness in others. This does not mean that we can trust everyone. There definitely are people who are mean or dishonest. But you have a better chance of influencing others to treat you kindly by perceiving them as kind.

The toughest people are often those who inside are small frightened children who have been emotionally wounded. View them with love and compassion and the fearful little child will feel more secure. A secure person can let go of a tough facade.

From now on be totally resolved to see people in a positive light. See beyond any outer crust of mud and soil. See beyond the negative facade. See the precious inner soul that is pure and holy. This vision has the ability to create miraculous transformations.

I was having a very difficult time with a few individuals. They were absolutely obnoxious when interacting with me. I tried smiling to them, but they just made fun of me. I consulted a warm and compassionate person who seemed to get along well with everyone.

"How are you able to get along with difficult people with whom so many others don't get along?" I asked him.

"I never meet difficult people," he replied.

"What do you mean?" I asked perplexed. "I myself have seen you in friendly conversations with difficult people."

"No one is always difficult," he responded. *"I see almost everyone as a caring friend of mine and that is how they respond. I still have to work on myself in this area. But I take responsibility for building up my positive view of those I still don't view in this way."*

39

BELIEVING IN PEOPLE

"No one ever believed in me. Because of this I was never able to believe in myself," complained an elderly man whose life had never amounted to much.

I wasn't a very successful student throughout my school years. But my mother kept telling me, "I believe in you. One day you will succeed." And I did, way beyond what anyone — besides my mother — ever thought I would. Her belief in me was a guiding light. I owe her everything.

I remember it like it was yesterday. I always wanted to be a writer. When I said this, most people laughed at me. "You don't have the talent to be a writer," is what I heard.

But then one day I confided in an experienced writer. "I'm embarrassed to say this because of the way others have reacted. I want to be a successful writer. Deep down I feel that one day I will fulfill my dream."

"Could you please bring me some examples of your writing," *she said.*

I did. And this was the best thing that ever happened to me. She pointed out some great sentences that I had written. "You still need a lot of practice and a lot of coaching. But I assure you that you'll make it big if you keep up your determination. Once you learn the craft, you'll excel."

And I did. Ever since then I look out for opportunities to encourage other writers. That is my biggest pleasure in life.

Believe in people and you will influence them to believe in themselves. Your belief needs to be based on reality. So develop an eye for noticing even sparks of ability that can be developed. Be enthusiastic in selling a person to himself.

Believe in youngsters and they will grow up with your belief as their internalized belief.

Believe in people who are starting out on a new venture and you will give them the courage they need to presevere. All beginnings are difficult, and your encouragement might just be what they need to withstand the inevitable storms and waves.

Believe in people's ability to make positive changes. Believe in people's ability to create a joyous life for themselves. And believe in your own ability to effectively change people by believing in them.

40

LEAVE PEOPLE FEELING BETTER ABOUT THEMSELVES

A valuable principle to keep in mind is: Leave people feeling better about themselves as a result of having met you.

Some people take pleasure in putting others down. It makes them feel more powerful to make others feel lower. In reality, the perpetration of such a crime lowers and demeans the perpetrator rather than the victim.

The person who leaves others feeling better about themselves elevates himself. The question to ask yourself is, "What can I say to this person that will give him a positive feeling?"

Be sincere in what you say. The goal is not to flatter or to give people a false sense of having a positive quality or attribute that they are missing. Rather the goal is to keep on developing your own "good eye" to see the positive in each person. When you develop positive feelings about other people, not only what you say will make them feel good but also how you say it. And not only will your words accomplish this, but so will the look on your face and your smile.

Use enthusiastic expressions. Instead of saying, "Not bad," you can say, "That was really good."

Instead of saying, "That was okay," you can say, "You're doing great."

Instead of saying, "That seems right," you can say, "That was very insightful."

Here are some other possibilities:

- "I admire your kindness."
- "I respect the way you handled that."
- "You have a lot of courage to do that."
- "That was magnificent of you."
- "I find you an inspiration."
- "There is a lot that I can learn from you."
- "You are so kind to have said that to me."
- "Your goodness is so much a part of you that you take it for granted."
- "Every time I see you I feel happier."
- "Whenever I meet you, I remember the kindness you have done for me."

I am now embarrassed to admit that I used to take pleasure in putting people down. I was a low-paid clerk at a nonprestigious job. It gave me a sense of being one-up to always say things that implied that I am superior and the other person is inferior. Even when I wasn't on the job, whenever some-

one told me about an accomplishment of theirs, I would say something to the effect that this was minor in comparison with what others had done.

I changed my pattern after meeting someone who told me that he made a resolution to always leave people feeling better about themselves. I tried to belittle this person in a number of ways. Then the person asked me, "Tell me the truth. How would you like people to feel after an encounter with you?" This wasn't really a question. We both knew what I was up to. From then on I realized that if I really want to feel good about myself, the way to do it is to make others feel good.

41.

ENHANCING SELF-IMAGE

T he way one views oneself is one of the most important factors in what one will accomplish throughout life. What you believe about yourself will either be conducive for living a joyous life or diametrically opposite. People with a low self-image severely limit themselves, and their entire quality of life will be lowered. They are more likely to be needlessly intimidated by what others say or think. They won't develop their skills and talents to their full potential. They won't accomplish as much as they would if they had a more enhanced self-image.

Self-image is a choice. It is a choice that is often not looked at as a choice. Our entire life history, especially our childhood, has a powerful effect on how we choose to view ourselves. The messages we heard from our parents about who we are had a major impact on us. The messages we heard from our family and close friends influenced us as did the messages we heard from people we met just once in passing. Some messages had a greater impact and others a more minor one. But all messages impacted on us. It is still our own decision about how we will view ourselves that is the key to how we define who we are.

While any individual can upgrade his or her self-image on their own, it is often more effective if an objective outsider shares with us a view of ourselves that enhances our self-image.

A person with a limiting self-image will not readily accept your positive statements. Just mouthing the right words, "I think you are a wonderful person," may or may not have meaning. First, you need to really feel that this is true. "Words that come from the heart enter the heart." Second, that person needs to be made to feel that what you say is valid.

When you say things to boost someone's self-image, he may respond, "You are just saying this to make me feel good." It's quite obvious that you're not saying this to make the person feel bad. But you must really believe and feel what you are saying. Then you can sincerely say, "I'm saying these positive things about you because they are true. And yes, I confess. I want you to feel better."

Believe in your own intrinsic value. When you have a deep and intense belief in the infinite value of each human being, the way you interact with others will automatically have a positive influence on their feelings about themselves. So every time you see your image in a mirror realize that you and every other human have fabulous worth. Integrating this yourself will enable you to spread this concept among others.

Be patient. Anyone who has had a low self-image all his life might not be open to making an immediate change in self-perception. At times one brief conversation might be the turning point for this person. Be prepared to have many conversations. How many? As many as it takes.

I recall seeing someone who radiated confidence and self-assurance in a modest way. This wasn't how he looked just six months before.

"You look great," I told him. "Did anything special happen to you?"

"Nothing that special," he replied. "But I did hear one sentence that was obvious, and somehow when I heard it this time it had a great effect on me. I attended a lecture and the speaker said, 'Your level of accomplishment is dependent on your self-image. And your self-image is whatever you decide it will be.' If it's my decision, then I will decide right now that my value to myself is infinite. I feel this now and I guess it shows."

42

FINDING STRENGTHS

Help people find their strengths. We all have more inner resources than we realize. If they lie dormant, they are like diamonds buried deep in one's backyard. The potential for wealth is there but it won't be utilized. So look for people's potential strengths and point them out in a way that is acceptable to them. These are strengths of memory and intelligence. These are talents and skills that can be developed into expertise. These are insights and creativity.

Once you express a strength in any area even once, you have the ability to upgrade that strength in more areas of your life many more times and in many more contexts. This means that if you have the courage to speak up even once you can speak up many more times when it is appropriate. If you can learn one word of a language, you can learn an entire language — if you are determined and patient. If you can be patient in one situation, you can be patient in many different situations. If you can concentrate while reading anything, you can learn to concentrate in many more contexts. Amazing, isn't it!

Once you believe that you personally can upgrade your strengths in all contexts, you can teach this to others. Theoretically you could teach this to others even if you don't apply it yourself. But if you don't exemplify what you expound, your message is not likely to be very effective. So applying your strengths in all contexts is a prerequisite for helping others to do so. This is one of the greatest gifts you can give your family and friends.

When people tell you that they can't do something, ask them if they have ever done this even once. "If you can do it once, it means your brain knows how to do it," you can tell them.

"Yes, but I have done this only in a limited way in another area," they might protest.

"Since you have already done this, if you do the exact same thing again, you are likely to get the same results, aren't you?" is your response.

And if you have helped even one person get in touch with one strength, you can get that person in touch with additional strengths. And if you have done this for one person, you can do this for many people.

I used to view myself as being uncreative. I remember the day a prominent neighbor told me that I was creative.

"Yes, I did a couple of things that might seem creative," I argued against my own best interests. "But I'm not really creative. And what I did wasn't totally original."

"Look at it objectively," I was told. "You have to admit there were elements of creativity in what you did."

He was correct. There were creative aspects in what I had done. And from then on, I have viewed myself as creative. This has made a major impact on my entire life. I now feel an obligation to help other people discover their strengths the way someone helped me find mine.

43

POSITIVE FEEDBACK

Some people identify themselves with their faults, weaknesses, and limitations. This weakens and limits them. Others identify themselves with their virtues, skills, and positive qualities. This strengthens them and brings out their best.

Identify yourself with your strengths and virtues. This will help you help others to do the same.

"What are your main strengths and virtues?" you can ask others. Some will feel comfortable telling them to you. Others won't. Some out of modesty. Others because they haven't as yet identified themselves with their strengths. When they do, it will feel so natural to them that they will readily mention it to others. It's not boasting but simply a statement of fact, similar to one's height or color of eyes.

Keep offering positive feedback whenever you can. The less a person identifies with his strengths, the more important it is for you to strengthen his identification with them.

Positive feedback is different than general praise. It is when you notice skill, talent, and excellence and comment:

- "That was very good."
- "I see that you are highly skilled at this."
- "Well-done."
- "This job was done with precision."
- "You do this excellently."
- "I admire your proficiency."
- "You are a true expert."

My parents criticized me, and rarely gave me positive feedback. I grew up feeling that I had many more faults than strengths. What changed my view of myself was a series of meetings I had with an empowering teacher. He pointed out strengths that I only barely realized I possessed.

"You are your strengths," he told me.

"But I hardly ever apply them," I argued.

"If you would apply them all the time I wouldn't have to reinforce your awareness of them," he smiled. "What really stops you from identifying yourself with your strengths?" he challenged me.

I thought for a moment and admitted, "The true answer is simply because I'm just not used to seeing myself that way."

"Experiment for an entire week," he suggested. "This week consider yourself a person who has these strengths. See the difference this makes."

I tried this for the week. It helped me so much that I kept it up. This was the single most empowering advice I had ever heard and it has made a major difference in my life.

44

VERBAL ENCOURAGEMENT

No matter how much you wish to help other people, you will be limited in what you can do for them. No one person has all the resources, talents, skills, and answers to help everyone who needs help. Even when you can't solve the problem, you can always give verbal encouragement.

Your verbal encouragement can be highly beneficial. Your verbal encouragement can help a person cope better until an actual solution is found. Your verbal encouragement can give a person the strength to continue to seek the help he needs. And your verbal encouragement might even enable a person to creatively find his own solutions.

Some people who can't help might defensively say things that embarrass or belittle a person who is already vulnerable. They say things such as:

- "Why can't you solve your own problems."
- "Why in the world would you think that I could do something to solve this?"

- "You're just lazy. That's why you are in this mess."
- "It's your own fault that you have this problem."

These patterns aren't helpful, to say the least. They belittle and cause discouragement. They can cause even more pain than was experienced before. In the words of someone who has suffered from this pattern, "I wish that those who can't help me would just leave me in peace. They cause me unbelievable torture. They don't know what it's like to be cross-examined by people who sound well-meaning, but in reality are tormentors. All they would need is one experience of this and then they would be much more careful about doing this to someone else."

Think about the outcome you want to achieve. You want the person you can't help to feel encouraged and hopeful. Speak only in terms that will create this outcome.

Here are some potentially beneficial patterns. Keep adding to them.

- "I'm sorry I can't solve this. I wish you tremendous success in finding a solution. If I think of anything, I'll call you."
- "My experience has been that many people with similar difficulties have found solutions. I'm certain that you will find one also."
- "I'll pray for you. I'll also speak to a few people who might be able to help."

I couldn't find a job. I was intelligent, but I lacked the skills and experience that would make me employable. I asked as many people as I could if they knew of a job opening. Some just said, "I don't know why you came to me. How should I know?" They made me feel just awful. This added to my anxiety about asking other people. Others didn't give the matter much thought and simply said, "Look at newspaper ads." Or, "Take a computer course."

I felt even worse when I was the recipient of a stern lecture. "How come you were so irresponsible and failed to get the proper training when you were younger? It's too late now. You should have been more concerned about your future. You have only yourself to blame." To say that this wasn't helpful would be a gross understatement. I felt bad enough about not having a job. I had no need of these painful speeches. If the people lecturing me would have had a minimal amount of empathy, they wouldn't have been able to say what they did.

Some people did give me leads that were reasonable possibilities. I was grateful for their trying. What I really appreciated were the people who listened to me and expressed sincere caring about my situation. Even though they didn't have a job to offer, they spoke to me in ways that gave me encouragement to continue my search. When I felt totally discouraged, I knew I could decrease the pressure by speaking with them. I wish more people would learn how to give encouragement. It's crucial to show a person whom you can't help that you understand him and truly wish him success. The people who did that for me gave me hope. May they be blessed.

45

THE WEALTHIEST CLIENT

D o you really want to learn how to treat another person with great respect? Then learn from business people and fund-raisers. Watch how they treat their wealthiest clients. Listen to how they speak. Observe what they do to give this person royal treatment. Then model these patterns with each person you encounter. Impossible to do?

Then at least do this with some people some of the time. And start with individuals who are least likely to be treated this way by others.

You never know. The very one whom you feel could never do anything at all for you might be a person who will transform your life. Today, he is penniless. At some point in the future, he might be wealthy. Today, he does not have clout. One day, he might be in a position to save your life. And even if he never has any money or never is able to do anything for you in a material sense, spiritually he elevates you.

Try this experiment. Each day for one week speak to one person as you would to the wealthiest potential client you will ever meet. Compare the difference in how you treat him now with how you would otherwise have treated him. This difference is what you need to work on to close the gap.

Recognize the spark of divinity in each human being. Your respect for the children of the Creator is ultimately the respect you show for the Creator.

Your personal honor is based on the honor you show others (*Ethics of the Fathers* 4:1). How honorable do you want to be? You might claim that it's important for you to consider yourself a valuable person. And if it truly is important then this will be manifest in how you treat others. Treating others with disrespect or contempt diminishes you.

Treating others with honor and respect elevates you. Elevate yourself. Treat others with tremendous respect and you instantly are higher than you were before.

You are independent of how anyone else treats you. You are totally dependent on how you treat others. Treat them as multibillion dollar clients and customers and your net worth goes up where it really counts.

When I was a teenager, I attended my cousin's wedding. His father-in-law was the head of a major yeshivah. I remember how he looked me straight in the eyes with great love and respect. That was 38 years ago. Every time I hear his name mentioned, I immediately think of the power of respectful eye contact. That is how people will remember you when your eyes express intense inner respect for others.

I am a fund raiser for a major organization. I had a meeting scheduled with a potential donor. At the meeting he told me, "I came by incognito yesterday to see how I would be treated by various staff members who didn't know that I was a potential donor. I want to tell you that I was greeted in a friendly manner and treated with respect. I noticed that everyone who came by was treated similarly. Your institution will benefit from this."

46

INCREASING CONFIDENCE

Lack of confidence is one of the biggest handicaps a person can have. Each handicap by definition limits us in some way. But many handicaps have the potential to strengthen our character. Growing from a handicap makes one great. Lack of confidence, however, weakens us. It prevents us from doing all that we could do and being all that we could be. Giving someone the gift of confidence will be the root of much good in that person's life. This is a gift whose benefits keep increasing as time goes on.

Help people become more aware of how they already have confidence in many areas. Ask them to list at least 10 areas where they feel confident. People who lack confidence tend to say, "I'm not confident." But the truth is that everyone is confident about a multitude of items.

I ask people who tell me that they aren't confident, "Are you confident that you know the entire alphabet?"

"Of course," is the inevitable reply.

"Are you confident that you can count from one to 20?" And

again obviously the answer is yes. There are many things that we know and can do and we just take them for granted. Every last thing that you know you know — and know that you can do — forms part of your attribute of confidence. Certainly you want to become more confident in other areas. So it's not that you aren't confident. Rather, you are making a goal to increase this valuable quality.

Those who lack confidence can be told, "Even when you don't know something, you can be confident that you don't know it. And you can be confident that with the right teacher and coach you will be able to learn many of the things that you don't yet know."

It can help to ask people whose confidence you wish to build, "Have you ever experienced not being confident about a subject or skill and then gaining confidence in that area?" We all have. If a person does not remember any instances right away, ask him to recall what he can do now that he couldn't do when he was born. He has already increased the amount of things that he is confident about. The same way that he already increased confidence he can keep on increasing this trait.

You might say, "If this sentence is true, please repeat it, 'I am confident that I can count to 10.'" After he repeats the sentence, you can ask, "You really are confident about this, aren't you?" Many people who say they lack confidence feel that they need to change their entire personality in order to be confident. When they repeat the sentence, "I am confident that I can count to 10," they experience the fact that confidence doesn't necessitate a major transformation of personality. "From now on," you can suggest, "view yourself as having confidence and as becoming increasingly confident all the time."

My parents were critical people and I grew up without confidence. I always felt that if my parents were less critical, I would have been much more confident. As I grew older I had a friend who also lacked confidence.

"My parents weren't critical of me," he confided in me, "but they were very bright and successful and so was my older brother. I was rather average and felt less confident than others who were equal to me in intelligence and talents."

We consulted with a professional to discuss methods of dealing with our feelings of inferiority.

"How would you like to feel?" he asked.

"Confident," we replied.

"What stops you from feeling this way?" he asked. We gave our diverse answers, blaming our lack of confidence on our parents.

"There's bad news and good news," he told us. "The bad news is that you are wrong, and the good news is that you are mistaken."

He noticed our puzzled faces, and continued. "The reason you lack confidence in the present is not because of your parents. It's because you have chosen to view yourselves this way and you keep making this choice. From now on start viewing yourselves as confident people. Think about all the things you are already confident about. Stand and walk the way a confident person would stand and walk. Look like a confident person would look. And speak with the tone of voice of a confident person. You can even say, "I don't know and I'll do research to find out," with total confidence. He added, "I believe that both of you already are more confident that you think. Keep thinking about how every act of confidence increases your confidence."

He called us from time to time to reinforce our becoming more confident.

My friend and I worked on this together. I knew we were successful when an old acquaintance who hadn't seen me for quite a while said to me, "You radiate confidence. What's your secret?"

47

HELP PEOPLE SET GOALS AND REACH THEM

One of the major keys to success in life is to make and reach goals. You can't reach a goal if you don't have one. So the act of making a goal or many goals is the first step to making things happen in your life. And if a person sets tremendous goals but doesn't do anything to reach them, he won't get very far. This is like sitting down and planning a world tour, but never buying a ticket to start the trip. Wishful thinking can be exciting, but unless you take action, you will remain where you were before.

When you make and reach goals yourself, you realize the vital importance and value of doing this. People who haven't made it a practice to keep setting goals can realize how important this is by thinking about how much more they could have done by setting goals and about how goal-setting has enabled others to achieve and produce.

Use your awareness of the value of goal-setting to inspire other people to do likewise. This one factor can help transform a person's life. I remember receiving a small pamphlet on goal setting from my friend Rabbi Kalman Packouz. It didn't say anything especially new, but since he went out of his way to send it to me,

I was motivated to delineate some major goals for myself. That was 20 years ago, and reaching those goals has made a major difference in my life. Reb Kalman, I am grateful and I thank you. You, the reader, will be the recipient of similar gratitude as you motivate and influence others to make and reach goals.

Keep asking, "Have you put your goals into writing?" Some will be open and share their goals with you. Others will prefer to keep them private. If a person doesn't have specific goals, encourage him. Highly motivated people may not need to write down their goals. They can visualize them written in their mind. For most people, however, it's preferable to write them down and frequently review them.

It helps to share one's goals with an encouraging friend or coach. Make it your goal to be there for others. You may be able to help others by encouraging them to make broader, more far-reaching goals. When a person is starting out in making and reaching goals, build up his belief in his ability to do this. Smaller goals lead to larger goals.

If a person seems hesitant about making goals, you can ask, "What stops you from setting goals?" By identifying the obstacles, you might be able to help this person overcome them. Some fear setting goals because they feel that they might not achieve them. You might say, "Setting a goal for which you were previously afraid to strive is progress in itself. Every goal for which you reach gives you greater knowledge about how to improve in the future. Your not succeeding is part of your life-education in how to have greater success in the future."

What are your goals for helping others set and reach goals? Put them in writing so they will empower you and help many others!

48

ACHIEVING DREAMS

M any of us have dreams that we would love to achieve but do not consider to be practical. We feel that our dream is so phenomenal that it would be too good to be true for us to make it a reality. A dream in its original form might truly be impossible. But we can take that dream and find ways to achieve its essence.

Helping people achieve their dreams does more than just help them reach their goals. They might have felt that something is impossible and you showed them how they can actually make it happen.

Consider this scenario. Someone lacks the money needed to pay for a course which will make a major difference in his ability to achieve his dream. You might give him the money as a grant, lend him the money with easy terms, or find someone else who would be willing to help out. You will be making a dream come true.

Or this one. Someone might have deep feelings about wanting a certain job, wishing to develop a certain talent, or dreaming to accomplish and achieve beyond what he or she thought possible.

You come along and find ways to make that want, wish, or dream an actual reality. This will help that person make a quantum leap. In essence, you will be creating a new person.

Never laugh at people's dreams. To you someone's dreams might seem as impossible as flying a machine heavier than air seemed to many before the Wright brothers' initial flight, or breaking the four-minute mile seemed before Roger Bannister did it. But those "impossible" dreams did come true.

If you feel that someone is wasting his time pursuing a truly impossible dream, be careful how you word your comments. Never mock anyone. Explain respectfully why you would advise this person to make changes in the exact form of the dream.

There are some dreams that might not be feasible in the original way they are presented. But there are aspects of those dreams that definitely can be reached. Someone might want to write a book that will totally change the world. Perhaps this is a bit too much. But a thousand people's lives might actually be changed. Not exactly the entire world, but a major accomplishment. And even the process of writing a manuscript that won't be published will change the author himself. As a teacher of mine used to say, "When you reach for the stars, you might not catch any, but at least you won't get your hands in the mud."

Keep asking people, "What are your dreams?" Some dreamers have learned from painful experiences not to share their dreams with others. They have been demeaned and ridiculed. Express your admiration and respect for the very act of having a dream. Be encouraging.

People who are hesitant about pursuing their dreams often have a feeling, "If I don't reach my dreams, I am a failure. So it's safer not to pursue a dream that might not work out." However, a positive action never results in failure. We learn something from each experience. One project leads to another. It's worthwhile working on 10 projects that don't make it. The 11th, 15th, or 20th project might be immensely successful. All the work devoted to the steps that led to the success retroactively will be seen as exactly what was needed to gain the necessary knowledge and experience.

If a person doesn't have a dream, you might ask, "If you weren't afraid to dream, what would your dream be?" By verbalizing a dream, the most important first step has been reached. And as you read this, you can ask yourself, "How can I actualize my dream to help others?"

49

"HOW HAVE YOU SOLVED THIS IN THE PAST?"

M any people who have specific problems have already solved similar problems in the past. When they are stuck in the problem, they are not in touch with how their previous actions can be utilized to solve it. You have a user-friendly tool to help them remember what they have already done before.

When someone is stuck in an unresourceful state, he is not likely to recall how he accessed and created more resourceful states in the past. You can ask, "Right now scan your entire life history and answer this question, 'What have you done in the past to access the state you wish to be in now?'" Or you can ask, "When have you felt this way before? What enabled you to overcome those feelings?"

If someone is having a difficult time interacting with a specific person, you can ask, "When have you interacted well with this person? What did you do then?" Or you can ask, "Think of a similar person with whom you have interacted well. What was your approach?"

If someone is in a slump in any area of his life, you can ask, "What have you done to overcome previous slumps?"

There will surely be new problems and new situations that this person has never before dealt with. Also, solutions that previously proved effective might not work now. But this is the easiest way to start.

Someone may have suffered from depression in the past, and is currently feeling depressed again. This state is not conducive to clear thinking. Whenever he experienced these feelings, he felt much better after running three miles and doing an act of kindness. The exercise cleared his mind so he could think about ways to solve the issues that were weighing on him. The acts of kindness made him feel better about himself. The question, "What have you done in the past to feel better?" will remind him of the benefits of his exercising and his acts of kindness. Another friend might have spoken with a specific counselor who was very helpful. At this stressful moment, he does not recall this. Your asking, "What has helped you before?" will remind him how much he benefited.

A friend of yours might usually be very creative. His creativity is the means by which he earns a living. He calls and says, "I think I lost my creativity. I haven't been able to think of anything original for over two weeks." Ask him, "Think of times in the past when you found it difficult to be creative. What exactly helped you regain it?" It might have been a brief vacation. It might have been a visit to a particular location where he could think clearly. It might have been a trip to a garden, a library, or a discussion with another creative person.

When I am speaking to someone who is angry at another person and wishes to overcome this feeling, I frequently say, "Think of a specific time in the past when you were angry at this person or at another person and let go of that anger. What did you think, say, or do to overcome that anger?" Since there are many approaches to overcoming anger, this enables you to find an approach that has worked for this person in the past and may very well be effective in the present.

A professional counselor who teaches non-professionals basic counseling skills related, "One of the first things I teach them is to ask people in a crisis, 'How have you solved a similar situation in the past?' One of the trainees said that he was faced with someone who was totally discouraged and didn't feel like living. At first the counselor felt that this called for someone with more experience. But then he remembered to ask the question. The person who was totally discouraged said that he had felt this way at least five times before. He elaborated on the different things that he had done in the past to revitalize himself. It was amazing how quickly this helped get him into a much healthier frame of mind.

50

POSITIVE ROLE MODELS

Your role models create you. They are your vision of what you wish to do and to become. They provide a clear picture of the measures to be undertaken to get there. Helping someone find an empowering role model will make a major difference in his life.

Some questions you can ask are:

- "Whom do you admire and respect?" "What specifically do you admire and respect about that person?"
- "If you could be like any specific individual, whom would you choose?"
- "If there were a few people who could teach you to be like them, who would you want to teach you?"
- "Whom have you met or read about that you would like to emulate?"
- "Do you have a secret wish to be like any great person?" If the response is no, you might ask, "If you would have a secret wish, what would it be?"

Read biographies of great people. They expand your mental

vision as to what is possible for you. After reading a biography, think about other people you know who would gain from reading it. You can have a powerful influence by telling someone, "I can see you being like this person in the future."

If someone confides in you and says, "I see myself eventually being like this great person," take heed how you respond. Don't belittle or ridicule him if you feel that this picture is too unrealistic. It's almost a certainty that this person's having a role model will enable him to accomplish much more than he would if he didn't have this role model.

For a while I would ask each person I met, "Who is your role model?" An interesting pattern developed. Those who were most successful almost all immediately listed their role models. Those who were less successful either didn't have one or would say, "I would like to be like this person. But it's definitely out of my reach."

This showed me the importance of influencing young people to find role models and of getting people to see that even if they won't exactly reach the level of their role models, following their role models will get them further than if they didn't have that picture in mind.

51.

ENCOURAGING THE DEFEATED

I ran for president of our organization. I had a good chance of winning and I kept visualizing the sweet taste of victory. I had a number of plans that I wanted to implement and I imagined vividly the steps I would take and the benefits to the whole organization. I pictured the smiles on the faces of my father and mother. I saw myself being congratulated by my family and friends. This was going to be the most exciting day of my life.

I was in for a big shock. My opponent received more votes than I did. The first few moments were quite easy. I felt totally numb. I even shook hands with the winner and offered friendly congratulations, adding, "I'm certain you'll do a good job." But then it hit me. I had lost. All my plans and dreams went up in smoke. I felt dejected and humiliated.

An older gentleman whom I greatly respected came to me the next day. "I know how you feel. I was once in a similar situation. I remember the shock and devastated feelings. For me this was the beginning of many accomplishments. It gave me a sense of humility and perspective. You are a great person and will accomplish a lot in your lifetime. It might take a while to get over it. Remember these feelings so you will be able to help others who have been defeated. Often the most successful people in world history were those who made comebacks after defeat. We can talk as often as you wish."

I was profoundly grateful. This speeded up my emotional healing immensely.

Say kind and encouraging words to people who have been defeated in any way. Losing can be painful. At times intensely so. Go out of your way to convey words of consolation. Write a letter, make a telephone call, send a gift.

Successful people know that every defeat is an added challenge. There are lessons to be learned. Defeat can strengthen your character. As you think about past defeats, continually grow from them. This will enable you to help others in a more effective way. Your own defeats are tools for spiritual victories.

Be careful not to just mouth platitudes. Feelings of compassion and empathy along with a simple, "I'm sorry," can be more powerful than more lengthy words uttered without feeling.

When you encourage people after they have suffered defeats, one day you will be told by a highly successful person, "I owe my success to you."

52

FROM SELF-CRITICAL TO OBJECTIVE OBSERVER

Whatever I do, I am criticized. When I make a mistake, I am told, "How could you have been so stupid?" When I speak to other people, I am frequently chided, "You are making a fool of yourself." When I do something right, I hear, "You should have done this a long time ago, and this is only a drop in the bucket of what you should be doing." It's torture to be consistently told off and put-down. And this criticism follows me wherever I go since it is my own inner voice that is doing the criticizing.

Saving someone from physical torture would be a deed of the highest priority. While being consistently verbally tortured is less dramatic, it is intensely distressful. Those who are excessively self-critical need someone from the outside to save them from themselves.

When you tell people who are self-critical to be more accepting of themselves, do so with sensitivity. You can just add to their distress by saying, "You are crazy for being so self-critical. Stop it already!" This is likely to make them self-critical about being self-critical.

Some people tell those who are highly self-critical, "This shows that you have a low self-image. If you had more self-esteem, you wouldn't be so critical of yourself." Great! Now the self-critical person has to worry about his low self-esteem. This definitely isn't going to lead him on the path to joy and self-acceptance.

People who are excessively self-critical often claim, "But if I'm not self-critical, I won't make positive changes." This is not necessarily true. When I type on my computer, the program I use immediately notifies me when I have made a typing error. I appreciate this feedback. To correct the mistakes, I don't need to say, "It was awful of me to make such a simple mistake. Don't you know how to spell such simple words? Won't you ever learn to do it right the first time." Making mistakes is part of the typing. You can correct the mistakes while feeling calm and relaxed.

Teach people to be objective about their mistakes, faults, and errors. Being objective about these things frees their mind to focus on what they need to do to correct them. Suggest that they internalize a sense of positive feelings about what they are doing wrong. "Now that I realize I was wrong I can improve."

I used to be consistently self-critical. My general state of being was one of anxiety. I was told by my parents and many other people, "You are too self-critical." My attitude towards those who said this to me was that they weren't serious enough about developing themselves. What changed me was that some-one I respected greatly told me, "I used to be just like you. I was never satisfied with myself. I knew that I could and should do better. But as I grew older I realized that a joyous attitude towards self-improvement was what I needed. Experiment for a month. Every time you realize you made a mistake, hear an inner voice telling you, 'It's great that I noticed this.' Imagine yourself rejoicing as if you found a great treasure. This changed my life and I think it will change yours." He was right, it did. I am on the lookout for people who seem to be as self-critical as I was. It is a high priority for me to help them become more objective about themselves.

53

STOP PUT-DOWNS

Stop people from putting themselves down. If a person has high self-esteem, but out of humility makes a modest statement, terrific. This is an elevated quality. But if a person whose self-image could use a boost needlessly makes a self-deprecatory statement, suggest gently that he doesn't need to and that it's not helpful.

Every self-inflicted put-down statement adds to a person's lack of belief in himself and his abilities. Many people who tend to do this need someone else to give them permission to stop doing it. Some do this so others won't blame them for being conceited or arrogant. True humility is awareness of your strengths paired with the awareness that they are all gifts. There is a difference between boasting and sharing your accomplishments with those who will be happy for you. Be careful not to cause envy or resentment. Strategic self-effacement can be advisable, but not if it is an expression of inferiority feelings.

Some people put themselves down to prevent others from criticizing them. They already criticize themselves so there is no need for anyone else to do so. And some people put themselves down so others will build them up. This can be an opportunity for an act of kindness on your part.

The following is a sample of statements which might be heard and the appropriate response:

- S: "I'm not so bright. But it seems to me that ..."

R: "You are entitled to state your opinion without commenting on your intelligence. And if your idea is good, that itself is an indication of brightness."

- S: "I'm so lazy. But I worked hard on this project."

R: "If you repeat that you are lazy, it makes it more difficult to overcome it. You have a right to tell me that you worked hard on this project without qualifying what you say."

- S: "I never do anything right."

R: "I'm certain that's an exaggeration. It is worthwhile to be more objective about what you do properly and what you don't."

- S: "I have a terrible memory."

R: "Fortunately you remember a vast number of things. Every time you do remember something, let it register that your brain has a tremendous storage and retrieval system."

- S: "I'm always putting myself down."

R: "It's great that you are doing so now. It gives me an opportunity to help you change this pattern. If you wouldn't always do it, perhaps I wouldn't be aware of it and couldn't help you change."

54

CHANGE: HARD WORK VERSUS ENJOYMENT

Your view of change will either motivate you to keep making positive changes or will make you fearful so you avoid change. One of the biggest changes a person can make is to go from viewing change as painful, hard work, to having an attitude of enjoying the entire process of self-development. While true change can be difficult, enjoying the process keeps you motivated.

Change is a natural process that begins in infancy. You changed when you learned to crawl. You changed when you learned to walk and run. You changed when you began to speak well enough for others to understand you. You changed when you began to read and write. You changed with each new skill you learned. And you changed when you internalized ideas and concepts that gave rise to your emotional states and actions.

What is your personal attitude towards change? The more you enjoy making changes, the easier it will be for you to help others view making changes as enjoyable. Learn from other people who enjoy making changes. Some teachers and coaches reframe change as painful and they reinforce this attitude in others. Find teachers and coaches whose greatest pleasure in life is self-development and growth. Ask them how they learned to enjoy this process.

When you think of making changes, think of the outcome: After you make the change how will you speak? What actions will you do? Keeping your mind on the outcome you want makes the process easier than if you keep thinking about how difficult it is to change from the way you are to the way you want to be.

Imagine how difficult it would be to walk if before each step, you would say to yourself, "It's so hard to lift my feet and defy gravity. With each step I take I once again need to overcome the powerful pull of gravity." Try it sometime. Then you will realize that taking 20 steps while thinking about going against the pull of gravity can be a difficult task. In practice, when we walk we keep our mind on the outcome and not on the difficulties involved.

Receiving an extremely large sum of money for making a change would make it much easier than not receiving that money. Why? When thinking about the significant benefits, one is highly motivated and the new actions are subjectively easier to do. So too with all changes. The more you focus on the benefits of a specific change, the easier it becomes.

I was lazy and pessimistic. I would always see the dark side of a situation. Nothing was so good that I couldn't find fault with it. I would blame and complain. My negativity caused misery to others and the one who suffered most was yours truly.

A number of people told me to go for counseling. I did. But I didn't feel up to spending months dredging up my miserable childhood and recalling every depressing memory. I was advised to ask potential counselors, "How do you view change?" Some responses were:

- *"How I view change isn't the issue. The issue is how you view change."*
- *"Change takes time and is very often very painful."*
- *"Most people don't have the inner fortitude to face the fact that they need to change."*
- *"We resist change. It takes a long time to understand and overcome our resistance. Then we can begin the long journey."*

Finally I met one who said, "Some changes can be painful. But by focusing on the benefits, the entire process will be meaningful and can be a source of joy in a person's life. I feel that most people can develop this attitude. We change all the time. Enjoy every positive step forward. Change really means that you are learning some new type of action and pattern of thought that will make your life better. This can be tremendously exciting." Meeting someone who felt enthusiastic about change changed me. It took a while to recondition my brain, but I enjoyed the process much more than I thought I would.

55

CORRECTING MISTAKES SENSITIVELY

When someone makes a mistake, he is vulnerable. It is an act of kindness to point out mistakes so they can be corrected. Correct others the way you would want to be corrected: with sensitivity. Both your tone of voice and the content of what you say should be as pleasant as possible.

Here are some of the ways not to correct mistakes:

- "That was a stupid mistake."
- "You never do anything right."
- "You just don't care."
- "You made similar mistakes a million times. How come you don't learn already?"
- "I'm surprised that you could botch up such an easy task."

If you attack the intelligence, skill, or caring of someone who made a mistake, you cause that person unnecessary distress. Such an approach is as big a mistake as the mistake of the person you seek to correct.

Here are some ways to correct mistakes:

- "I've made similar mistakes myself. This is what I've learned concerning how to ..."
- "You probably realize it. You just need to ..."
- "That happens to many people. Then they learn to do it this way ..."
- "I'm sure you know how to do it right and that this was an oversight."

I have a sensitive nature. I hate to be put-down or verbally attacked. I don't like making mistakes, and I appreciate the opportunity to correct them. I feel that some people enjoy catching me on mistakes. They seem to take pleasure when they can pounce on me and shout, "That was wrong." You would think that the people who try to correct me with such glee would be more open to accept correction themselves. My experience is that those who attack most fervently are the most likely to be defensive about their own mistakes. They deny whenever they can. And when circumstances prevent them from denying their mistakes, they blame others or come up with all kinds of far-fetched excuses.

I think that if the people who most readily correct others would correct them sensitively, they would be more open to accept corrections themselves. One who sincerely wants to correct others will be motivated to find the most effective patterns.

I used to be insensitive to the way I corrected others. Then one day at a public meeting someone embarrassed me in front of a large crowd.

"You idiot!" he screamed. "You've got your facts wrong."

I felt humiliated. At that moment I sincerely resolved to correct others as gently as I could.

56

UNDO THE "CURSES" OF NEGATIVE PREDICTIONS

"You'll never amount to anything."

"You won't be able to cope with such a difficult situation."

"You're too stupid to understand."

"No one will marry you, and if some unlucky person does, your marriage will be a disaster."

Many people carry an invisible burden. This is the weight of unfavorable predictions about their abilities and future. These "curses" are usually a product of someone's frustration, anger, resentment, or spite. At times well-meaning parents, teachers, or friends will deliver their negative prognosis in the form of giving advice.

You have the ability to undo these curses. You can point out the limitations of the people who gave those negative forecasts.

Some of the things you can say are:

- "No human being has the right to limit another person. Whoever tries to limit you is wrong."
- "You already have learned so much. Keep it up and this trend will take you much further than anyone could foresee."
- "This person was just speaking out of anger. An angry person makes mistakes and spouts untruths. He doesn't know what he's talking about."
- "There are others with far less natural intelligence, talents, and skills who have coped well and accomplished much. You will too when you persist in utilizing your positive attributes."
- "Don't give up. If you quit, you will be defeating yourself. But if you utilize all your inner resources, I guarantee that you will succeed in the end."

Experts in a field can have the experience to make positive predictions:

- "I've been teaching for 30 years and I believe that you have the intelligence to do well."
- "You have what it takes to cope well. I've seen people who couldn't and I know that you can."
- "I've met people with greater handicaps who have put in the effort and have accomplished greatly."

When you meet people who aren't doing well in some area, interview them for potential negative predictions. "What were the messages your parents and teachers gave you about your abilities and future?" "Has anyone ever told you that you wouldn't be able to succeed?" Use your knowledge, experience, and creativity to help transcend and transform counterproductive predictions to ones that are helpful and beneficial.

It's easy to issue limiting predictions. It can be difficult to undo their effects. If someone has internalized a negative picture, it can take a lot of effort on your part to counteract it. Be persistent. Your success will help transform this person's life.

57

COUNTERACTING A NEGATIVE MEDICAL PROGNOSIS

I was told that I had only a few days left to live. That was over 40 years ago.

Several doctors told me that we would be unable to have children. Fortunately they were wrong.

My doctor told me that I had only one chance in 500 of overcoming my illness. I think he was being generous by giving me one chance. I used hope and laughter and spent the rest of my life encouraging others to believe in their ability to recover, just as I did.

D octors are humans. And all humans make mistakes. Those who feel they never make errors are guilty of an extreme error. Doctors save lives and heal. But they are fallible. Doctors have a mandate to heal, not to give up. Many doctors respect this mandate. Some don't. They can mean well and in their minds don't want to give false hopes. But a pessimistic prognosis can create discouragement. It is incumbent upon doctors to qualify a negative prognosis. They do have a responsibility to tell someone that a situation is serious and proper medical treatment is warranted. But it is crucial for them to be aware of instances when people did recover even though it might have appeared to be unlikely. The greater a doctor's knowledge of exceptions to the standard, the greater his ability to soften a dire pronouncement.

Hearing and reading stories about people who have recovered from life-threatening illnesses will supply you with ammunition to fight depressing medical statements. We need to live in reality. But it is a major error to prematurely feel that all hope is lost when there is a valid basis for that hope.

Medical miracles do happen. People who were not given a hope for recovery have recovered. Even those who do not fully recover often live many more fruitful years than an original prognosis predicted.

Recovery and healing can happen with serious medical conditions. All the more so with psychological and psychiatric disorders. Being told, "Your problem is deep-seated and you'll never live a happy life," can create a self-fulfilling prophecy that can greatly hinder someone's ability to regain emotional health. Give hope and encouragement when someone has been told, "Nothing can be done."

"Nothing can be done," really means: "At the present with my limited knowledge and abilities I don't know what I can do to help." It doesn't mean that no one else can help. And it doesn't mean that this very person won't be able to help in the future. And it doesn't mean that there won't be spontaneous remission.

A helpful sentence is, "You never know."

- "You never know. Perhaps the situation is better than you think."
- "You never know. You might recover and be healed."
- "You never know all the good you can still experience."
- "You never know how spiritually elevated you can become by coping with this situation."

58

SAVING MONEY

One aspect of caring about people is respecting their property and protecting their money. Be mindful to return lost objects, to give suggestions about how to buy things economically, to prevent damage to possessions, and to prevent needless waste. Your caring for the material and financial concerns of another person is a matter of your spirituality.

If you see that someone has left his possessions unguarded in an area where they might be stolen, bring them to a safe place and then explain that it's wise to be more careful.

If you personally have had some loss through negligence or through the dishonesty of someone else, use this as an opportunity to help save others from similar loss. This can be a helpful reframe. "My personal loss puts me into a position where I can do an act of kindness for others." The more people you help, the greater the benefit you have from your original investment. True, this wasn't an investment that you willfully decided on. But once you have had your experience, the distress will be minimized by the knowledge that you are able to help others in ways that you wouldn't have thought of without your own loss.

If another person is upset over a certain loss that he had, you might be able to suggest ways whereby he could help others with his experience. You will be helping both the person who suffered this loss and all the people whom he will help by warning them to be careful. He will now be able to feel a bit better about his own loss, and your suggestion will have caused other people to gain also.

If there is a special sale that you know will really save people money, think of who would benefit and contact them. This is especially important if you know that a specific person or family is challenged financially.

If you read an article that shows how to avoid loss of any kind, pass it on to others who could also benefit.

When I first married, an older couple came over to our house for a visit. They gave us a treasury of tips on how to make purchases as economically as possible. My husband and I were extremely grateful. We lived on a tight budget, and their advice and suggestions were exactly what we needed. Later on, I found out that they did this regularly for new couples who moved into their community.

59

"STOP HARMING YOURSELF"

Imagine someone who is totally discouraged. For a while now nothing has been going right. Everything in his life is falling apart. With each blow he becomes more deeply depressed. He has no energy left. He's not eating and not sleeping. Thoughts of putting an end to it all become stronger. He's walking near a bridge. Below is a turbulent river. It's tempting for him to jump. As he's contemplating this drastic decision, you walk by. He looks to you as his last chance. "Do you think I should jump?" he asks. Here's your opportunity to save his life. You will use every persuasion tactic and strategy that you can possibly think of. His life is up to you and you will do whatever you can to save him.

Not everyone is approached by people contemplating suicide. But we all encounter people who are harming themselves and putting their lives in danger. Did you ever see anyone smoking a cigarette? These "coffin nails" are certified to be dangerous. Did you ever see someone crossing a street without looking both ways carefully? He is asking for trouble. Did you ever see someone driving excessively fast or passing another car in defiance of basic rules of safety? This person might end up killing his family, innocent strangers, or even himself.

Whenever you see someone doing something that is potentially harmful to himself or others, speak up. Use the persuasion abilities you have stored in your mental library and influence this person to stop doing things that are harmful and potentially destructive.

What if you have no inkling of how to motivate people in these situations? Learn how. Read. Take a course on selling or persuasion. Consult experts for advice. Do whatever you can to gain the necessary knowledge. Saving a life is the greatest act of kindness. Make it a priority to learn how.

I am forever grateful to the person who successfully insisted that I go on a diet. I was obese and was consistently gaining weight. "Diets aren't for me," I thought. I tried many of them but didn't have the willpower to carry through. Then someone who barely knew me said to me with total compassion, "Do me a favor. Let me save your life. I'll speak to you daily and give you encouragement to stick to a healthy diet." This person called me up two and three times a day. When I asked how I could repay this kindness, I was told, "Just be there for someone else like I was there for you."

60

THE POWER OF "WHY?"

"Why?" One word that can elicit so many different reactions. When you ask someone "Why?" you can enlighten or frustrate. You can find new insights or cause defensiveness. A curious "Why?" asker can be an inventor, a brilliant researcher who finds medical and technological breakthroughs. When you keep asking yourself, "Why?" you will gain considerable self-knowledge that will enable you to gain a greater understanding of your own motivations and reactions. The question "Why?" can also cause a person to rationalize, to invent farfetched reasons that have no basis in reality even though someone thinks they are accurate, or to willfully state a good-sounding answer that is blatantly false.

Help people understand themselves better by asking them "Why?" questions. An important warning!! Only direct "Why?" questions to people who appreciate them. Refrain from asking such questions when they would be considered an invasion of privacy or would cause irritation and anger. Using "Why?" wisely and compassionately, however, will enable people to get in touch with their values and drives. An honest answer to "Why?" teaches us what motivates us. At times it will enable a person to realize that blocks, fears, and apprehensions have no real foundation and then they will no longer be a source of anxiety or limitation.

For example, if someone is worried and you keep asking, "Why are you worried about this?" he might realize that what he is worrying about is unlikely to happen. You might ask, "Why would that be so awful?" and the person can see that it really wouldn't be so awful. If someone is afraid of public speaking, your asking, "Why are you afraid of speaking to people?" might show him that the fears are greatly exaggerated. Then he will find them easier to overcome.

Some people will gain a lot by asking themselves, "Why?" But they won't feel comfortable sharing their inner thoughts with others. If so, suggest that they ask themselves "Why?" questions. Since they will keep their answers private, they will find it easier to be honest with themselves about why they are doing the things they are doing. This can influence them to refrain from doing things that are counterproductive. And they will be able to elevate their motivation if they find that they are doing the right things for the wrong reasons.

When you are doing kind acts, don't allow an imperfect reason to prevent you from further kind acts. Some people might realize that they are acting kindly because they want to be liked or are afraid of the anger of others. Some might do kindness for the approval and honor they receive. It's preferable to do kindness with ulterior motives than not to do kindness at all. The goal is to keep doing the kind acts, and to elevate your reasons for doing them.

The "Why?" questions of a counselor changed my life. I had some issues to work out and I consulted a professional. The first thing he asked me was, "Why are you here?" I told him what I considered to be the real reason. He kept asking me again and again: "Why are you here?" I delved into myself and the insights I gained enabled me to create a much more meaningful life for myself and my family.

If anyone asks you an annoying "Why?" question, you have a number of options as to how to reply. Some are:

- "Why not?"
- "Why do you feel a need to know?"
- "Why is that important to you?"
- "That's a good question. I'll think about it."

 Or simply,

- "I would prefer not to answer."

61.

THE POWER OF "WHAT?"

Utilize the power of the "What?" tool:

- "What can I do for you?"
- "What do you really want?" (Said in a tone that conveys the message: "I want to meet your real needs.")
- "What do you need to make that happen?"
- "What inner resources that you already have would enable you to accomplish more?"
- "What changes would you like?"

R epeat these five questions until they become automatic for you. The best way to repeat them is to ask them frequently to others who would appreciate them.

The previous section dealt with the power of "Why?" questions. There are many instances when "What?" questions are much more preferable. At times, "Why?" questions will get people even more stuck than they were before. "What?" questions can shed light on what needs to be done to improve a person and correct a situation.

For example, "Why are you the way you are?" and, "Why do you have this fault?" can bolster the strength of limitations and faults. Compare that with asking:

- "What can you do to improve?"
- "What would motivate you to overcome that fault?"
- "What thoughts, attitudes, and beliefs would improve the emotional quality of your life and enable you to experience more joy?"
- "What actions can you take that would help you make the changes that you would want?"
- "What strengths would you need to create new and better patterns of behavior?"

Advocates of using more "What?" questions than "Why?" questions have calculated that it can take as much time to answer a "What can be done now?" question as it would to answer a "Why am I limited or stuck?" question. Even after you know why you are as deficient as you are, you still need to do something about it. So if a "What?" question will do the job, it's not a worthwhile investment to spend too long a time on the "Why?" question.

At times, only by knowing why something is the way it is, will we be able to figure out what we need to do now. Then, of course, it's imperative to answer the "Why?" question before trying to solve the issue of "What should I do now?"

Some people spend months and months, even years, trying to

understand why they are the way they are. They use this as an excuse for not changing. "I'm the same as I always was," they proudly say, "But now I know why I am the way I am."

The "What?" question to keep foremost in our mind is: "What can I do for this person?" You might not always come up with an immediate answer. But being on the lookout for what you can do will inevitably enable you to find things that you wouldn't have noticed or realized without having asked this question.

62

WHAT STOPS YOU?

"What stops you?" This is a valuable question to ask yourself and to ask others.

"What stops you from doing more for others?" If the answer is that you are already at the limits of your resources of time, money, and energy, that means you are willing to do more as soon as you have greater resources. If, however, the answer is laziness, a need for comfort, selfishness, not caring enough about others, or not even thinking about the issue, you will now have a sense of direction for what you need to do to become more of a giver. When you ask this of yourself, you might prefer the wording, "What stops me from doing more?"

"What stops you?" Pose this question to others who would like to do more than they are presently doing in any area of their lives. There might be major obstacles that are blocking them from doing more or there might be minor obstacles. Being clear about the exact nature of the obstacles is a major step in overcoming them. Often, people don't think about the exact nature of what stops them. They just know that they don't, won't, or can't do something. Now that they think about the specifics of what stops them they will find it easier to find ways around, over, and under those obstacles.

If a person is stopped from doing positive things because of a lack of knowledge and information, help them get that information. You might have that information yourself. If not, you might know who can be consulted. You might know of books or pamphlets that supply the necessary information, or you can suggest ways to acquire those books.

If a person is stopped because of fear or anxiety, you might be able to alleviate that fear by showing the person that things will be much easier than he thinks. You might have had the same types of fears and were able to overcome them. You might be able to give the person so much encouragement that he now will have the confidence and courage to do what he was hesitant to do before. Ask him how he overcame past fears. Ask him about times when he was afraid to try something but when he actually tried the fears vanished. Ask him how he coped with difficulties in the past. Show him that he will benefit so much from what you are suggesting that it's worthwhile facing those fears head on and not letting them get in the way.

If a person is stopped from doing more for others because of self-centeredness, explain how the good that one does for others is the greatest good that one can do for oneself.

I wanted to continue my studies but because of financial pressures I felt unable to. A friend of mine tried to convince me that it would be in my best interests to start a study program. To me this seemed overwhelming and I meekly responded with an, "I can't."

"What stops you?" my friend asked me. I told him a number of reasons. Once he heard the specific objections, he showed me how I could overcome each obstacle.

This general pattern of calmly identifying the objections and dealing with them has made his life immensely successful. I am just one of the many people whose lives he has helped make more meaningful.

63

SIX KEYS TO MOTIVATION

Motivation. Whatever you do, you do it because you are motivated. Whether or not you help others to your utmost will depend on your own level of motivation. The more motivated you are, the more you will do. Motivating others to do life-enhancing things and teaching them how to motivate themselves will help them in every area of their lives.

I have written (in *Anger: The Inner Teacher*) that there are six terms that are key elements in motivating ourselves and others. These terms are in three categories: (a) Right and (b) Wrong. (c) Gain and (d) Loss. (e) Pleasure and (f) Pain. Memorize them and repeat them frequently. They will point the way to find factors to motivate yourself and others.

(a) When you feel that something is the right thing to do, you will tend to do it. (b) When you know clearly that it is wrong to do something, you will tend not to do it. It's easy to rationalize and tell yourself that what you know is wrong isn't really that wrong. But deep down you know it is. Also, when you know that it's wrong not to do something, you tend to do it.

(c) When you will gain from doing something, you will tend to do it. (d) Similarly, when you know that you will lose out by not doing something, you tend to do it.

(e) When doing something is pleasurable, you tend to do it. (f) When doing something is painful, you tend not to do it. And when it would be painful for you not to do something, you are likely to do it.

The way to increase the amount of kindness you do is to increase your realization that it is the right thing to do. We live to fulfill a mission in life. Part of your mission is to do what you can for others. It is wrong not to do the kindness that you are capable of doing. This is especially wrong if someone will suffer by your failure to do this kindness. You gain immensely spiritually and emotionally when you do acts of kindness. The life of a person who does acts of kindness for others is much more fulfilling and meaningful. You lose out on this by failing to do acts of kindness for others. The more pleasure you personally experience when you do acts of kindness, the more likely it is that you will increase the kindness that you do. Even those who don't feel this pleasure right away, eventually will. They will get feedback that they have helped the lives of others. The more pain you have from the suffering of others, the more likely it is that you will do what you can to spare others from pain.

When you want to motivate others to do something, (a) show them that what you are suggesting is the right thing to do, (b) it is wrong not to do it, (c) they will gain by doing it, (d) they will lose by not doing it, (e) they will have pleasure from doing it and

(f) they will have anguish if they don't do it. In some instances you will immediately see the relevant factors on which you can focus. In other instances, you might need to be a little more creative. You can add your own reward system so the person will gain by doing what you are suggesting. When you are persistent and keep repeating your suggestions, the person might find your persistence more difficult to take than what you are asking him to do, so he will do it just to stop you.

There are unlimited variations when you think about using these six concepts. Use them wisely and benevolently. They can be the catalyst for much good. People who aren't motivated to do what they can in life, are wasting the most precious commodity they have. By motivating them, you are literally saving their lives.

A person who is highly skilled in motivating people related, "I personally am motivated by the knowledge that what I am doing is the right thing. So when I try to motivate others, I tend to think that all I need to show them is how this is the right thing and they will run to do it. Reality has taught me that not everyone works this way. I now try to find as many ways as possible that a person will benefit and gain from doing what I suggest. I am now able to motivate people that I previously wasn't able to budge."

64

MAKING PEACE

"Be a disciple of Aaron: Love peace and pursue peace" (*Ethics of the Fathers* 1:11). This principle of the renowned Sage Hillel is beautiful. When there is peace, there is harmony, there is cooperation, and people do things to benefit others. Peace eliminates the harm and damage caused by its opposite: quarrels, fighting, anger, resentment, hatred, revenge, grudge-bearing. Creating peace adds to people's lives and saves everyone involved from the pain and destruction of feuds and quarrels.

Being a peace-maker is an art. And it is fraught with danger, so one must be very careful how one goes about the whole process. We are taught that Aaron had a special method for making peace. When he heard that two people were quarreling, he would approach one and tell him that the other person was saying positive things about him. He would then approach the second person and tell him that the first person was saying positive things about him. The next time they met, their body language said, "I like this person." This created a positive loop and the two people would once again become friendly with each other.

We like people who like us and speak well of us. When you want to make peace between people, skillfully have each one say something positive about the other. "What has this person done for you that you have been grateful for?" "What positive qualities do you see in this person?" "If you weren't angry at this person, what positive statements do you think you could make?"

Describe how they both will benefit by getting along well with each other. Past grievances often have to be worked out. But not always. At times, two people will be willing to begin their relationship all over again. They can be shown that it's best to begin again right now. When there is a need to speak about the past, caution everyone to avoid speaking in a tone of voice and with content that will be inflammatory. They should speak to be understood, not to attack. Have each one listen quietly to the other. This can be extremely difficult. But by not counterattacking and by not being defensive, the speaker has the relief of being heard and understood.

By speaking about the situation peacefully, both parties might recognize that they misunderstood the actual positions of the other. They might not have realized the pain the other one experienced. They might have thought that the other person was purposely trying to say and do things to cause them pain. Now they will each see that the other person was just trying to do what he thought was best for himself, and didn't really want to cause harm and damage.

Whenever possible find an agreement frame. That is, find points on which they agree and have common interests. "What do you both agree on?" "If possible, you both would gain from getting along well with each other, wouldn't you?" "If you worked together instead of against each other, that would make life easier for you, wouldn't it?"

If you are serving as a mediator, be careful not to take sides. Often, each party will want you to agree that they are right and the other side is wrong. If you are an authority and a judge, this could be appropriate. But when you are serving as a mediator, be careful not to become a party to the dispute. Instead of finding a peaceful settlement, you will then expand the quarrel. The side that feels you are against them will now need to look for other people to bolster their position. The quarrel will grow instead of resolving itself peacefully.

You will be most successful when you can perceive both people in a positive light. When you can create a positive atmosphere in the room by radiating good-will to everyone involved, both parties will be able to express themselves in a peaceful setting. Your presence will enable them to understand and be understood in ways that they would not have been able to if you weren't there.

But be very careful not to make the situation worse. You might be close friends with both parties and they both want to win you over. You might say something that one can use as ammunition against the other. They might be better off finding someone who is an objective outsider to serve as a peace mediator.

If you do everything you can and tempers still flare, realize that there might be deep emotional issues that have been around for many years. The resentment has added up and now it explodes. You might have to speak to each one separately to enable them to calm down before they can speak to each other. There might be hidden issues that one or both are not telling you. You think that you know the entire picture, but important pieces of data that you aren't aware of would change the way that you are looking at the situation.

Know your limits. Know when you should step out of a situation. Know when your involvement will cause havoc with your emotions and drag you into something in which you didn't need to be involved. At times the only way someone will know these limits is to have been involved in trying to help out in a quarrel that blew up in his face. When you know what you can't do, you will have more time and energy to be involved in what you can do.

I was once involved in a complex situation where a professional lawyer with many years experience was brought in as a consultant to the case. He sat back and listened carefully to get as comprehensive a picture as possible.

In the middle of the presentation he was repeatedly getting asked, "What do you think so far?"

He replied, "Thus far I'm still trying to get a more complete picture. I don't have any comments yet."

Only when the picture became very clear did he make his comments and state his opinion. Because of his extensive experience he knew that things are not always as they seem. Two sides in a quarrel will each have a different perception of the situation and it takes patience to get the entire picture.

65

ENHANCING MARRIAGES

"You could have done better." The mother who said this to her son caused marital strife and friction for many years to come. Five powerfully destructive words.

"What a jewel you have." These five words created a beautiful marriage. Both the husband and wife viewed one another as precious diamonds. The man who was told this had viewed his wife through critical lenses. Then someone he respected said this to him.
"Are you serious?" he asked.
"Of course," he was told. "You are married to a very special person. Treat her as a diamond and she will reciprocate." He did, and she did.

Be on the lookout for what you can say to a married couple that will enhance their marriage. Even people who love and respect each other dearly can use positive feedback.

Be careful. A couple that is having serious difficulties interacting with each other might react with cynicism if your praise is too profuse. You might say, "You are married to a wonderful person," and what will go through the mind of the recipient will be, "You don't know what you are talking about." In such situations mild praise on a specific positive action would be preferable.

In my book *Marriage*, I have elaborated on how to enhance a marriage. Here are a few ideas that you can pass on to a married couple:

- Apply outcome thinking. That is, before you say or do something, ask yourself, "What will be the outcome of what I will say or do?" Only say or do things that are likely to have positive outcomes.
- See the good. Focus on the positive deeds, qualities, and patterns of your spouse.
- Don't cause pain. Give pleasure. These five words create positive marriages.
- Reframe positively. Find positive ways to evaluate what your spouse says and does.
- Apologize first. Take the initiative to apologize for any mistakes, misunderstandings, or wrongs.
- Focus on your own responsibilities. Don't blame your spouse for not being all that he or she should be. Rather, focus on your own responsibilities to be loving and respectful.
- Speak with respect at all times. Even if you are upset or angry, still speak with respect.
- Build your character traits as you build your marriage.
- Constantly say and do things to put your spouse in positive states.

66

"IT WILL BE ALL RIGHT"

When someone is concerned or worried about the future, some people tend to give a general reassurance, "It will be all right." If the individual you say this to becomes calmer, what you have said was beneficial. But often global statements of, "Don't worry," or, "It will be okay," won't relieve someone's concerns, nervousness, or anxiety. When a person with much experience says, "It will be all right," the recipient of this statement knows that there is a valid reason for assuming that things will be well. When, however, this is taken as a dismissal of their concerns without facts or experience to back it up, it usually isn't very helpful.

Address the specific issues that are bothering the person who is worried. Show him how things are likely to work out. Share your own experiences with him as well as the experiences of others in similar situations that worked out well. Do research and find the relevant reassuring data. Tell him your plan of action and how this can solve the problem. Explain how even if things don't work out exactly as he would wish, he still will be able to cope with the outcome.

When speaking to a worrier, ask, "What exactly are you worried about?" When you first heard about someone's worry, you might have assumed the worry was about one issue, but that was not the worrier's real concern. Regardless of how much reassurance you gave on that issue, it wouldn't work. This person needs reassurance on another issue. By finding out what exactly is bothering this person, you will be able to really help him and not just say something that sounds good but won't do anything for him.

I used to be a major worrier. I would try to lessen the distress of my worrying by telling other people how worried I was. I often heard generalities such as, "There's nothing to worry about." "Trust that all will be good." "Think good and it will be good." For many people this worked wonders. But not for me. I had to go underground with my worrying.

It was like a miracle that I met someone who told me that he too had been an obsessive worrier. He worried about anything that might possibly go wrong. Now he looked like anything but a worrier. As a matter of fact he was one of the most serene people I had ever met. When he described how he used to worry, it made me feel so much better. I was only an amateur compared to his description of himself as a professional worrier. He told me the thought patterns that had helped him.

"I think about the worst case scenario," he told me, "and I accept it. I think about potential solutions. I pray. I analyze the probabilities of what I worry about actually occurring. I increased my ability to focus on the present, which is much

easier for me to handle than the future, which is always unknown. I began to visualize happy endings to the things I worried about. Since worry is only in my imagination, I create much more enjoyable pictures in my mind. I worked on gaining greater mastery over my emotional states. I learned to reframe the potentially negative into more positive evaluations. I sought to make the best out of problematic situations."

He spoke to me for several hours. The point that helped me the most was his sharing with me how he was an ex-worrier. I knew that what he told me was valid. I had living proof that the ideas he used actually worked. Since they worked for him, they would work for me. I now try to help every worrier I meet. Utilizing my own worrying as a resource to help others overcome their worrying has given me a positive reframe for all of the suffering I had endured from worrying.

67

EMOTIONAL STATES ARE CONTAGIOUS

Whatever emotional state you are in will have an effect on the people you encounter. The best way to spread joy is to be joyous yourself. The best way to spread compassion and kindness is to be in a compassionate state yourself. The best way to spread serenity is to be in a serene state yourself.

Just after writing the above paragraph, as I was on my way to deliver a lecture, I encountered two people who were in very different states. One was highly agitated. He was begging for money and it was clear that he had serious emotional difficulties. I was very aware of how this person's agitation had an effect on my state. Within two minutes, I encountered someone who was in an entirely different state. This person's oldest brother was getting married the next day. He was in a happy emotional state, looking forward to the joyous wedding. I walked away in a state of celebration. Both encounters lasted about a minute and both strongly affected my own state.

Mastering your own ability to access your best emotional

states at will enables you to have a positive effect on others. Even if you have what would be considered a difficult encounter with others, when you remain calm and clear thinking your state will begin to calm them even before the content of what you say will reach them.

In my book, *Happiness*, I have dealt with how to gain greater mastery of one's states. In general, the more practice you have of accessing states at will, the easier it will be for you to access your best states even in complex, difficult, and potentially hostile situations. The states of being centered and balanced, serene and compassionate will enable you to interact with others at your best. Keep practicing your ability to remember times and moments when you were in these states. Keep learning from role models who are in these states to see and hear what they look and sound like. Practicing in front of a mirror will give you feedback as to how you look when you are in your different states. This makes it easier for you to transform your states by changing your facial expressions and body language.

As you master your own emotional states, eventually your very presence will be an act of kindness. When people are around you, they will feel more joyous and more serene — and they will feel better about themselves in general.

I had a teacher who radiated such positive feelings about life and other people that as soon as he walked into our classroom, we all felt that we were in the presence of a special light. He himself had a difficult life, but one would never know it.

When you spoke to him, you were the total focus of his attention, and you felt uplifted and inspired. My goal was to emulate him. I remember the first time someone said to me, "I feel so much better about myself as soon as I begin to talk to you." This person's feedback was extremely helpful to show me that I was on the right track. I'm not always in the state that I wish to be in. I am resolved to gain greater mastery of my own states because of the good that this can do for others.

68

TEACH ENTHUSIASM

Give a person enthusiasm and you have given him a key to success. Enthusiasm isn't everything, but it goes far.

When a person goes for a job interview, all things being equal, enthusiasm will give him a better chance of getting hired. Enthusiasm without knowledge and skill won't accomplish. But an enthusiastic person is most likely to gain the necessary knowledge and skill. By helping someone increase his level of enthusiasm, you increase his potential for success when meeting new people.

Enthusiasm is energy. And energy is what you need to get up and go. Unfortunately, there are many of whom it can be said, "His get up and go has gotten up and gone." Don't let that be said about you. Be enthusiastic about increasing the enthusiasm of others.

When enthusiasm is faked, it's likely to be incongruent. It can be overdone. Some people will still appreciate it. "At least he's trying." Others might be put off. There is external enthusiasm that increases internal enthusiasm. This is when you sincerely want to be enthusiastic, but you aren't spontaneously in this state. By acting externally the way you want to feel internally, you will increase your inner enthusiasm.

What are you spontaneously enthusiastic about? Ask this of yourself and of those you want to help increase their level of enthusiasm. Remember your most enthusiastic moments. Recall what you saw. See that vividly now. Recall how you sounded when you spoke with intense enthusiasm. Feel those feelings once again. By being able to access the state of enthusiasm at will, you will be able to transfer this to others.

If you try to teach someone to be more enthusiastic when you aren't in this state yourself, you are lacking an important ingredient. Still, you can never tell. You might be able to say to someone, "Personally, I find it difficult to feel enthusiastic right now. But even if I can't do it, you still might be able to."

Model enthusiastic people. Find people who are highly enthusiastic. Interview them and find out what thoughts and attitudes enable them to be enthusiastic. Practice talking the way they talk. Mirror their body language.

The same way that you will experience more enthusiasm by mirroring enthusiastic people, so too you can help others become more enthusiastic by mirroring you when you are enthusiastic. Speak about something that you are enthusiastic about and ask the person you wish to inspire to mirror you. Have him speak in the same manner about something that arouses his enthusiasm. Keep giving him feedback about his tone of voice and body language.

Build up your own enthusiasm for doing acts of kindness. And do what you can to influence others to be enthusiastic about doing acts of kindness. This will have a powerful effect on many lives as the chain reaction keeps spreading.

69

CHEERING THE GRUMPY

Wouldn't the world be a much better place if all the grumpy people would be transformed into kind, loving, and cheerful human beings? Those individuals would gain immensely along with all of the potential victims of their negativity.

Imagine telling a grumpy person, "Cheer up," or, "Stop being so grumpy." Will this suddenly change them? Will they stop being grumpy and cheer up? If it were that simple, we'd live in a cheerful world. A group of volunteers would go from person to person and change them. It's obvious that cheering up a grouch is an art and a skill.

There is no magic formula that will work in all instances. But the most effective approach is when you have sincere love for other people. When you care deeply about someone and have sincere compassion you are likely to have a positive effect. Even the grumpiest of people can melt when in the presence of the radiant sunshine of a sincerely loving person.

Don't rebuke a grumpy person. It won't work. Don't angrily

tell him to change. It won't work. Enter his world. Understand him. Why is he the way he is? What pain in his life caused him to be this way?

If you try to cheer up a grumpy person and what you try to do doesn't work, don't blame him. Take this as a message that you need a different approach.

If you act too friendly and cheerful when interacting with a person who is consistently grumpy, you are likely to annoy him. One approach is to mirror his grumpy state and then change your state in a way that makes him want to follow you as you access a better state. Mirror but don't mimic his facial expression and posture. Mirror his tone of voice, but don't say anything that will be counterproductive. Then little by little allow yourself to relax and little by little access a slightly cheerful state. If he follows your example, you will put him in a better state.

I once met a cheerful person who seemed to have grown up with this attribute.

"You probably were always a happy person," I commented to him.

With a big smile, he replied, "I'm afraid not. I was a difficult child. I kvetched a lot and was frequently miserable. As a young adult I was highly irritable. People usually got on my nerves. One day, however, I met someone who had a major impact on my life. This person said something humorous and made me smile.

"You have a great smile," he said to me. "You should see how

different you look when you smile from the way you look without that smile. Look at the difference in a mirror. Start with smiling. Speak cheerfully to each person you meet. Experiment for an entire month."

"So far my experiment has lasted over 10 years and I think I'll keep it up for at least another 10 years."

70

HAPPINESS-PRODUCING QUESTIONS

When you ask people questions, you get them to focus on specific pieces of information and memories. It's an act of kindness to ask the type of questions that give people pleasure and increase their level of happiness.

Here are some questions that you can use as tools to help people access positive states:

- What gives you the most happiness in your life?
- What were your greatest moments?
- What are your favorite childhood memories?
- What are some of the nicest things that people have said to you?
- What was your best vacation?
- What makes you smile?
- What makes you laugh?
- Who makes you feel good just by being in that person's presence?
- What do you enjoy reading?

- What songs put you in positive states?
- What is your favorite possession?
- What is your favorite day of the year?
- When have you unexpectedly had a better time than you thought you would?
- When have you been pleasantly surprised by the way something you did turned out?
- When did you feel you would succeed and you actually did?
- When have you felt joy about seeing someone you hadn't seen in a long time?
- What praises and positive feedback have you appreciated?
- What is the nicest thing a teacher ever told you?
- When did you surprise yourself by being more skillful at something than you thought you could?
- How do you look when you smile at yourself in a mirror?
- When has someone given you a gift that you greatly appreciated?
- What do you consider your wisest decision?
- What advice do you have for others to increase their happiness?
- What did you do for someone else that you felt great about?
- What is the nicest thing a total stranger ever did for you?
- What have you been grateful for in the past?
- What are you grateful for in the present?
- When have you felt joyous for no special reason?
- What healthy activities give you a natural high?

- When were you about to give up and someone's encouragement kept you motivated?
- (For grandparents): What is a clever thing one of your grandchildren said?
- What is your favorite question from all that have been asked of you?

71.

TEACH "NO"

Many people need to learn to say "yes" more often. Others need to learn to say "no." The more kind acts you personally do, the more your telling someone to develop a balanced perspective will be accepted.

Some people say "yes" out of embarrassment when they would prefer to say "no." At times they know they should say "yes" to a request, but they are feeling a bit lazy. However, fear of embarrassment motivates them to live up to their ideals and it is therefore a positive force in their life.

But when they really don't have the energy or time to do some positive thing they need permission and encouragement to say "no."

Help them. You might say, "You really don't have the energy right now. Look for a future opportunity when you do have the energy." Or you might say, "Right now your plate is full. You have an exhausting schedule. By saying 'no' now, you will be able to say 'yes' many times in the future."

Some people are intimidated by the anger of others. "If I don't agree to do what this person asks me to do, then he will get angry at me." Anger is often used as a manipulative device. Those who use anger to get people to do what they wish, have learned that others feel so uncomfortable in the face of anger that they do what they wouldn't do otherwise to placate the angry person. If you are not in physical danger, don't allow someone's anger to control you. Encourage others not to be blackmailed by anger. Train yourself to remain calm and centered in the face of anger. Then teach your skill to others. It's important not to say anything to an angry person that will just get him angrier. Speak softly. Think before you speak. Only say that which will effectively soothe the angry person. You might be able to say, "If your request is reasonable, I will try to meet it. But please state your request pleasantly."

I was becoming totally overwhelmed. I felt that any time anyone asked me to do something for them, I had to agree to do it. It became known that I was the one to ask for all types of favors. I love doing things for others, but too much of a good thing can be a problem. I was constantly tired and exhausted. I still feel guilty that I wasn't doing even more. Finally, I became so run down that I collapsed.

An elderly kind-hearted soul visited me when I was recuperating. I told her how badly I felt that my not feeling well prevented my doing for others. After questioning me about my hectic schedule, she said to me, "I insist that you learn to tell people that you would like to help them, but can't. When you can say 'no,' your 'yes' is a real yes." I respected her for her good deeds and accepted her opinion. From then on I was more balanced on what I agreed to do and what I declined.

72.

MISTAKES

I've tried to help people in various ways. But unfortunately I've made mistakes. I've introduced people to each other and in the end they didn't get along. I've tried to give people advice and things didn't work out as well as I thought they would. I've tried to get people jobs, but in the end they were dissatisfied. I feel like leaving well enough alone. Why should I try to help people if it will cause them suffering and they will have complaints against me?

The only way you will avoid all mistakes is by not doing anything. But then you won't accomplish anything. "There is no one wiser than a person with experience," goes a well-known saying. Learn from your mistakes. They are an integral part of your course on becoming an expert at helping people.

If we would wait for a surgeon with a perfect record, many lives would be lost because highly competent physicians wouldn't operate, since they were imperfect. If only perfect teachers were allowed to teach, there wouldn't be very many schools. If only financial advisers whose advice has proven infallible were allowed to practice even the most brilliant financial analysts would have to look for another job. Expertise is within reach, perfection isn't.

If someone asks you for advice and there are other people who are more qualified to give it, defer to those people. But when you are qualified, don't allow lack of infallibility to stop you from helping others.

View your mistakes as the price you pay for preventing future mistakes. Be honest about your mistakes. Some people fear mistakes to such a degree that they always claim they were really right. They are so afraid of mistakes that they defend whatever they do as having been the best plan of action. This is a normal reaction, and it takes integrity and courage to transcend it. Let the knowledge that you are developing your character make it easier for you to acknowledge mistakes.

I used to be totally devastated if I made a mistake when trying to help another person. I truly wanted to alleviate the suffering of as many people as possible and to help people improve their lives. I felt a tremendous amount of guilt and embarrassment if what I said or did was counterproductive. The turning point for me was when I needed the help of others. When they sincerely wanted to help me and did all they could, I didn't expect them to be omniscient and omnipotent. I accepted the outcome as a matter of Divine Providence. This realization gave me the inner strength to learn from my mistakes and to continue being there for others.

73

BE PREPARED FOR COMPLAINTS

I can't believe it. Before I was devoted to helping others, very few people had complaints against me. It seems that the more I do for others, the more people are upset with me. Those I help, complain, "Why aren't you doing more?" Those I am unable to help complain, "How come you help other people and not us?" Those who are angry with me for various reasons tell me, "You feel that just because you help people you don't have to live up to other obligations."

When you devote your life to helping others, you are likely to arouse envy, animosity, and resentment. The needs of the people you help can be so great that they will be angry you aren't helping them even more than you are. Your energy, time, and other resources are limited, so those you don't help might feel resentful that you do more for others than you do for them.

Some people will be envious of the good you do. In order to feel better about themselves, they will find it easier to put you down than to do more themselves. They are likely to challenge your motivations:

- "He only helps others because of his overblown ego."
- "She only helps those whom she feels will help her."
- "He wants to get ahead politically so he does favors for others."
- "She only does kindness because she is compensating for feelings of inferiority."

Even if these claims aren't true, cynical or envious people are likely to make them. Someone with mixed motives — he wants to help others but he does enjoy honor — is likely to feel more hurt about this than someone whose motivations are pure. However, anyone who has a sensitive nature can feel hurt.

Being criticized is part of the price one pays for helping others. This elevates you: You are willing to personally suffer in order to do acts of kindness for others. Acknowledge the truth of a complaint and it will be easier to tolerate.

- "Yes. I should do a lot more than I am doing. I'm sorry that I'm limited."
- "I acknowledge that I am only doing a drop in the bucket compared to what needs to be done."
- "I agree that it would be wonderful if I were doing more than I am."
- "Yes. I am inconsistent. But I feel it's better to continue doing the good that I'm doing than to consistently do nothing for others."

I remember how shocked I was when someone whom I have

helped greatly told me off in great anger, "You aren't there for me enough when I really need you. Okay, so you did help me before, but what about lately!"

After this I heard about being prepared for such occurrences. The next time someone I had helped attacked me for not doing enough for him, I was mentally ready to answer with true compassion, "I'm sorry for not being there when you needed me. I see how much you've suffered. It's really rough."

The amazing thing is that when I said this with sincere concern, the person's anger subsided and I received an apology. My response was, "That's all right. I understand the pressure you were under." We parted with good feelings.

74

SPEAK UP FOR YOUR RIGHTS

I'm afraid that if I view myself as a kind person, I will have to give to others all the time. I am happy to help others whenever I can, but I don't like the idea of having to give in to the demands and requests of anyone who wants anything from me. If I find myself in a situation where there is a conflict of interest between what I would like and what someone else would like, do you mean to tell me that I should always give in and never assert my rights?

We definitely have a right to stick up for our rights. But always do so with respect for the other person.

If you have a question about whether or not it would be proper for you to act in a certain way, consult with an objective authority. But in principle keep in mind that we are not obligated to give in to the unreasonable demands of another person. Even if a demand is reasonable, if you will suffer a loss you don't have to automatically give in. Since there will be many dilemmas in these areas, it is imperative to find a wise and experienced authority to consult.

Some people find it difficult to speak up for their rights. To overcome their reluctance to do so, they might react with out-of-character aggressiveness. It is exactly their tendency to avoid speaking up for themselves that could cause an angry outburst. Speak pleasantly and respectfully when negotiating for your rights.

While no one wants to be taken advantage of, for some people it is a super high priority not to be considered a sucker. The very thought of being taken advantage of makes them shudder with mortification. It is important for them to make it an equally high priority not to speak disrespectfully to another human being.

When claiming your rights, be careful to do so with a pleasant tone of voice. Even if you are upset, make an extreme effort to speak in the way you would wish to be spoken to.

Some ways of expressing yourself are:

- "Perhaps you didn't realize it, but I was here first."
- "I'm afraid that I can't agree to this."
- "I hear your request. But at this time I am not able to say yes."
- "I'm sorry. The terms that are offered do not make it worth-while."
- "I'm certain that if you were in my shoes, you would likewise turn down the offer."
- "I would like to give you what you want, but circumstances don't allow for it."
- "Please don't do that again."
- "I appeal to your sense of justice and fair play. Please respect my rights just as I will respect yours."

I would let others treat me like a doormat. I felt that I was doing the righteous thing. Then an elderly scholar who saw me being taken advantage of told me, "Every situation is a test of our character. Even how we speak up for ourselves. Failing to defend your rights would be a sign that you don't feel good enough about yourself. Sticking up for yourself aggressively isn't proper. Be assertive and be persistent. And do it all with a sense of mutual respect."

Hearing this from a righteous person gave me the knowledge that I had a right to defend my rights. Even though I was strongly criticized by my adversary, I realized that he was speaking from his bias, rather than stating a valid position.

75

BEING TAKEN ADVANTAGE OF

There is a well-known story about two friends who hadn't seen each other for over 20 years. They were excited about finally meeting again. They had much news to share and great memories to reminisce about. The one whose city they met in went into a store to make a purchase.

"Good morning, Joe," he said cheerfully to the owner of the store. "I hope that you have a wonderful and great day."

The owner of the store just grunted.

After paying for what he had bought, he once again blessed the store owner, "Have a fantastic day, Joe. And may you be successful beyond your wildest imagination."

Again, the owner of the store just grunted.

"He must be in a bad mood today," the visiting friend commented.

"Why do you think so?" his friend asked.

"Because of the way that he responded to your cheerful blessings."

"Oh, this is the way he always responds. I've been buying

things here for years."

"Then why are you so friendly towards him?" the visiting friend asked.

"I wish this person well. But I don't want him to be my teacher when it comes to greeting people."

Some people have a real fear. They never want to be taken advantage of. And it's definitely appropriate to be careful not to be cheated or deceived. The Sages (*Deuteronomy* 22:4; *Rashi*) define being taken advantage of in this way: People ask you to do something that they could really do themselves, but they are lazy and want comfort. Our obligation is only to help someone who is carrying a load that he can't manage on his own.

When you are kind to someone who is not kind to you, you are not being taken advantage of. You are acting in an elevated manner. This is where the Torah prohibition against taking revenge and bearing a grudge applies (*Leviticus* 19:18). Suppose your neighbor never lends you anything of his. If he needs to borrow something that belongs to you, it is forbidden to refuse to lend it to him. He is not supposed to be your role model of a kind person. Perhaps if you are consistently kind to him, you will eventually influence him to become a kinder person himself. But even if he never changes, you need to be kind in order to accomplish your mission in this world. And the more difficult it is, the greater is your kind act.

Since being kind to someone who fails to be kind to you can be a great challenge, mentally prepare yourself to pass this test of being a truly kind person. Visualize yourself being asked for a loan or some other favor by someone who consistently refuses to lend you anything. Vividly picture yourself being joyous as you lend this person what he needs. Run this over and over again in your mind until you feel that you will be able to carry it out when the opportunity arises.

76.

DON'T BLAME PEOPLE FOR NOT FOLLOWING YOUR SUGGESTIONS

I give wonderful advice to people in many different areas. I tell people who have financial difficulties what they can do to increase their incomes, yet they don't do a thing I advise. I tell people how to increase their level of happiness, and they don't try the exercises I suggest. I tell them how to get along better with other people, and they stupidly repeat their old patterns even though they don't work well. I want to help, but most people are resistant to change. When I tell them it's their own fault, they just become angry at me and don't take the responsibility themselves to improve their lives.

When you try to help others and they don't listen to you, you have a choice. You can blame them for not being more open: "They are resistant and it's impossible to help them." Or, you can view the situation from another angle and say that you are not yet as proficient at influencing and motivating this individual as you need to be.

A blame-free attitude is the best path to choose. This can motivate you to develop your skills and talents on how to persuade, influence, and motivate. As you enhance your presentation skills, in the future you will influence others to follow your beneficial suggestions.

Focus on the benefits of what you are advising this person. Show him how he will gain from following your suggestions. Find out what stops this person from following your suggestions. You might ask:

- "What stops you from trying this?"
- "What objections do you have to what I said?"
- "Is there anything about this that bothers you?"
- "What would you need to know in order to test this out?"

If he is afraid to try, perhaps his reasons are valid. He isn't you and you aren't him. It's possible that your suggestions would be perfect for you, and a disaster for him. You can never know the entire picture.

When a person would like to follow your advice, but is apprehensive, do what you can to help him overcome his fears. Perhaps he doesn't have a clear picture of what he needs to do. Help him develop that picture. Teach him the steps that he needs to take. Perhaps he just needs time to get used to the ideas you are suggesting. If you feel certain that what you are suggesting is in his best interests, perhaps you can repeat your suggestions at a later time. Then you might be able to better present them, or this person might be more open to listening to you.

77

DON'T USE A HATCHET

There is an old saying, "Don't use a hatchet to remove a fly from your friend's forehead." In the literal sense this isn't common. But figuratively many might be guilty of doing what the saying warns not to do.

Removing a fly from someone's head is an act of kindness. But don't do anything that will make the situation worse for the person you are trying to help. The first rule in helping people is: Do no harm!

One form of this pattern is when you try to influence someone to improve in some way, but what you say causes discouragement. Telling someone, "You are so lazy you'll never get anywhere in life," won't motivate this person to become noted for his alacrity and proactivity.

Telling someone who made a mistake, "Why can't you learn to do things right?" makes an assumption. It's giving the person a message that he can never learn to do things right. If he really can't, there is no benefit in your asking this question. If he really can, then your question is acting as a barrier to prevent him from learning better ways to do things.

A parent or teacher who punishes a child, yells and shouts, and causes pain because of a child's failure to study properly, can easily cause a child to form negative associations about studying. The intention might be for the child's best interests. But the approach will intensify the problem rather than solve it.

We are most likely to be guilty of using counterproductive approaches when we become angry at someone we care about for not doing things that will be helpful to him or for doing things that are harmful. Ironically the more we care, the more likely we are to become angrier. And the angrier we are the less clearly we think. We need to keep our original intention in mind. We care and that is why we react. So let what you say and the way you say it reflect your sincere care. The message you convey should be, "You are important to me and I care about your welfare."

When I was a young girl, my mother would try to motivate me to eat by saying, "Think of all the starving children in the world who would be happy to eat this food." My feeling sorry for those children took away my appetite.

When I didn't do my homework, my teacher would embarrass me in front of the entire class. This didn't make me love to do homework. Instead it made me hate the subject that teacher taught.

I didn't call home very frequently. Whenever I did call home, the first reaction I heard was always, "How come you didn't call until now? Why do you make us worry so much about you?" This made me feel guilty. But I so disliked hearing it that I kept pushing off making telephone calls to my parents. I wish they would have said, "We're so happy to hear from you." This would have made me call more often.

When my friend told me about mistakes he made, I used to react, "How could you have messed up such an easy thing?" He wanted my suggestion about what to do to prevent these mistakes in the future. Only later did I find out that my reactions stopped him from confiding in me.

78

"JUST" JUST WON'T WORK

- "Just don't worry."
- "Just smile and be happy."
- "Just stop getting angry."
- "Just refrain from that bad habit."
- "Just do what you should do."

Just telling someone what he just should or just shouldn't do will usually not be effective. Even so, at times just a short remark just might work. But don't count on it.

When someone feels overwhelmed, telling him a brief "just" remark will usually be insufficient. When someone is furious at another person, telling him, "Just calm down," usually won't have a major effect on his emotional state. If someone is addicted to some substance or to a bad habit, telling him, "Just don't give in to it" — and expecting it to work like magic — is usually a bit naïve. When someone is consistently lazy and lacks motivation to take action, saying anything in the "just" family is not likely to transform him into a proactive, energetic, dynamo.

"Just" sentences imply that it's easy. They imply that the person knows exactly what needs to be done and all he has to do is make a slight effort to apply what he knows. "Just" sentences don't take the person's subjective feelings and emotions into account. Many people have great intentions of creating positive habits and overcoming negative ones, yet they find it extremely difficult to make actual changes.

When you say a sentence beginning with "just," you are likely to be giving a message that you lack the patience and persistence to keep on helping this person until the problem is resolved. The solution might actually be easier than this person thinks, but you are likely to lose rapport if the person you try to help doesn't think that you truly understand the underlying feelings and difficulties.

It's tempting to try to get by with a "just" sentence because it's a lot easier than trying to develop a personalized program that will be effective for the person you are trying to help. But knowing what won't work is beneficial. For then you will continue your search for a viable plan.

When I feel stuck and share my feelings with those whom I feel might help me, I hate it when they tell me pat answers. The content of these statements shows me that the speaker is well-intentioned, but doesn't have a clue about what I really need. If a person doesn't know what to say, I'd appreciate his listening so he can understand and then say sincerely, "I'm sorry you're having a rough time."

When other people had difficulties with habits and patterns that I had mastered, I used to tell them, "Just do this," or "Just don't do that." But with experience I've learned not to say this to most people. I now say, "I see how much this is weighing on you. I'd love to be able to help you. I'll keep thinking about it. I realize that it isn't easy. Perhaps you might experiment with this approach ..."

79

DON'T CONDESCEND

Have a deep sense of respect for anyone you help. The people you help are helping you fulfill your life's mission. Be grateful to them. Be especially careful not to speak or act condescendingly when you try to help someone. The good you do can be offset by the damage caused by the condescension.

I have been having financial difficulties. Some people have lent me money in such a way that I felt they believed in me and trusted me. Others have refused politely. I respect the way they have done so. Some people have refused to help me and they've done so by questioning my honesty and integrity. I can't describe the anguish they caused me. Yet others have helped me out, but did so in ways that made me feel inferior. Everything about their verbal and nonverbal communication has given me the feeling they look down at me. If I hadn't been desperate for financial help, I would have refused to borrow their money.

When I need to ask people for information, some answer me in a manner and tone of voice that says loud and clear, "I consider you dumb and stupid." They probably don't realize how much they hurt me. In contrast I've met brilliant scholars who have made me feel important and valuable regardless of how simple my question was.

I encountered someone recently who said to me, "I remember how inferior and inadequate you used to feel. You're fortunate for having met me. I made you into what you are today." He seemed to have a strong interest in putting me down in order to feel good about himself.

I needed private lessons to catch up on what I didn't understand. Someone offered to teach me. I was apprehensive because of negative experiences I've had in the past when people have taught me privately. But the way this person spoke to me gave me the feeling that he had a basic respect for the dignity of each person he taught. He told me that he too had many areas that were difficult for him, while others had much more of a natural skill in those areas.

"And furthermore," he said, "our brain is a total gift. Not one of us did anything to create our own brain. Even the biggest genius can end up with his brain ceasing to function. I'm grateful for the way my brain operates, and I have an obligation to help others with the resources that I've been given."

He emphasized that I had emotional intelligence and a spir-

itual goodness. He made me feel so good about myself that my mind was open and clear. I gained more from him than I did from anyone I had studied with before.

I heard the story of a person who wanted to give money to a street beggar. This beggar sold a few pencils to create the illusion that he was selling something and not asking for a free handout. Most people who gave him money just dropped their coins in his can. But one man carefully inspected the pencils and took the one that looked the best.

"I'll buy this one," he said to the man on the street, looking him straight in the eye while he nodded his head in respect and gave him a smile. From then on the erstwhile beggar had a greater degree of self-respect and decided to start a real business. I am reminded of this story whenever someone asks me for a personal donation. I hope that my respect for others will help them attain greater dignity and self-respect.

80

DON'T USE YOUR KINDNESS AS A WEAPON

"I have done so much for you already. You are a rotten person for not doing what I want you to do now. You would be nothing without me, do you realize that? If I would have known that you would fail to repay me in kind, I wouldn't have done for you all that I have done. As much as you could possibly do for me, it's minor in comparison with what I have done for you."

Some people use their kindness as a weapon. When they are angry towards others they have helped, they attack those people with the kindness they have done for them.

Never use the good you have done for someone as an offensive weapon. Once you have done the good, it's ancient history. You have gained eternally from the spiritual benefits of your kindness. Don't destroy your merit by trying to destroy a person you have helped.

If you want to use a past kind act as leverage to motivate someone to help you, do so with respect and dignity. Some people will not bring up past kindnesses even if the receipient of those kindnesses refuses to help them. If, however, you do feel a need to mention a past kindness, don't even imply that you regret your kind deed. The value of that good you have done is too precious to be negated.

Some people you have helped might be embarrassed to be reminded of this in the future. If this is possible, be sensitive to the feelings of those people and don't even hint at your having been their benefactor in the past.

My friend told me that he once witnessed an elderly man, who was the head of a charitable organization, being berated by someone he had helped greatly a number of years earlier. The angry person kept yelling and shouting insults. The kind man remained silent and just apologized for having been the source of this person's distress.

My friend later asked that elderly gentleman, "You did so much for this person. Why didn't you remind him of what you did for him? Perhaps that would have calmed him down."

"First of all," he replied, "this person had a need to vent his angry feelings. I don't take such things personally. He suffers a lot and I was glad to be able to help him let off steam. Secondly, once I do something for someone, I prefer not to remind him of it. He doesn't owe me anything for what I have done."

81

TEN DON'TS

[1] DON'T be obsessed with the people you can't help. Focus on the people you can help. You are a mortal. You, like everyone else, are limited. Obsessing about what you can't do prevents you from thinking about things you can do.

[2] DON'T let the lack of kindness and giving of others influence you to stop helping and giving. Some people feel resentful, "Other people aren't helping. Why should I?" We learn from role models. Learn from those who are kind, not from those who are not.

[3] DON'T keep trying to help someone who truly doesn't want your help. Some people are very independent. They could gain from accepting your help, but their need to be on their own is stronger than their wish for your help. Be aware that some people really want your help but are embarrassed about it. If you feel that this is the case, try to say things to put the person at ease.

[4] DON'T give up too soon. Some people might think that you really won't be able to help them so they initially tell you not to bother. If you don't give up, both you and the other person will see that he will gain much more than he thought.

[5] DON'T complain that other people keep asking you to do things for them. If others come to you for help, it's an expression that they believe you are a kind person. You might not be able to meet other people's needs right now, but by being aware of their needs, you might think of a creative solution.

[6] DON'T tell anyone, "I had to go without this for a long time. So you also can go without it." Other people have a right to something even if you didn't always have it. If you don't want to help someone, just say a polite, "No."

[7] DON'T be hurt if a selfish person complains that you are selfish. Some selfish people try to manipulate kind, giving people by telling them they are selfish. Perhaps you are being selfish. Then again, perhaps not. You might want to ask objective outsiders for their opinion.

[8] DON'T be naïve. Don't believe every story you hear. If a story seems questionable, check it out. If you have good reason to believe that someone is lying to you, perhaps he is. But be very careful. Someone's sad story might not at first seem true, but it could very well be that it is. A person who loves kindness would

rather err on the possibility of helping someone who doesn't need it rather than not helping someone who does.

[9] DON'T say things that might cause someone to feel badly when you help him. Some people might say things such as, "This is so difficult for me to do. I don't know why I agreed to do it for you." Or, "This is the last time I'll commit myself to do this for anyone."

[10] DON'T embarrass someone when you do something for him. Be careful not to say or do anything in the presence of others that would cause distress to the person you are trying to help.

82

FIND SOMEONE WHO CAN

W hen you can't help someone yourself, assist that person by finding someone else who can and will. Be aware of resource people who appreciate helping others.

Someone who is housebound or in the hospital might need visitors. If you can't do it yourself, find people who are able to visit and influence them to do so.

- Someone who is deeply in debt needs help to raise large amounts of money. This problem could be beyond your personal ability to solve. Perhaps you can find some people who will be able to financially bail this person out of his distressful situation. Or, you might know someone you can ask to advise this individual about what he can do to raise the necessary funds.

- Someone complains to you that he is having a very difficult time with his children. You might know a person who is knowledgeable about how to handle these situations. If you don't know someone who can help, you might know someone who knows someone else who can help.

- A group of individuals can get together to compile a list of resource people for solving various difficulties. They can then spread the word that their pooled knowledge can be accessed by calling specific telephone numbers.
- Larger cities might have many more resources than smaller towns. People who live in a place with few resources can refer others who need the information to contacts elswhere.

A general rule to remember is: As soon as you realize that you can't help someone in need, think of some people who might be able to help. You might not be able to think of someone the moment you are asked, so keep it in mind or write it down. Then as soon as you think of a resource person, you can contact the person who is seeking assistance. Imagine the relief of the person you help when you contact him a few weeks later to pass on helpful information. He sees that you have been thinking about his welfare all this time.

When people used to ask me to help them out in some way, I had an attitude, "There are some things that I am able to do and others I am not able to do. When I can't do anything, that's it. There's just nothing I can do." What helped change my attitude was when I needed a referral for a computer expert who could help me with a nonstandard problem. Most people told me that they couldn't help and left it at that. Then I happened to bump into a total stranger who said to me, "I have a friend who might be able to help. Give me your telephone number." He spoke to his friend who was able to help. This incident has served as a lesson for me. I now look for others who can help when I can't.

83

EVERY TIME ...

- Every time you act kindly, the world has more kindness.
- Every time you are compassionate, the world has more compassion.
- Every time you smile to someone, the world is a more cheerful place.
- Every time you help transform someone's worry into serenity, the world is a more serene place.
- Every time you calm someone who is angry, the world is a more pleasant place.
- Every time you give money to charity, the world is a more charitable place.
- Every time you encourage someone to do something for others, you are creating a partner to make a better world.

Some people spend way too much time complaining about the awful state the world is in. There is too much aggression and violence. There is too little kindness and compassion. There is too much anger and depression and too little serenity and joy.

If someone complains and complains, the world is still full of whatever it is the person is complaining about, and now more complaining has been added. Conversely, if someone spreads compassion and kindness, the world improves. The ripple effect can spread these positive qualities. A little positive action is more beneficial than a mountain full of complaints.

- Every time you visit someone who is ill, you are making the world a kinder place to live in.
- Every time you comfort a mourner, you are making the world a kinder place to live in.
- Every time you judge someone favorably, you are making the world a kinder place to live in.
- Every time you lend one of your possessions to someone, you are making the world a kinder place to live in.
- Every time you help a stranger find his way, you are making the world a kinder place to live in.

What emerges from all this is that there is no such thing as an insignificant kind act, because every time you do an act of kindness you are elevating the world we live in.

84

"I'VE BEEN WAITING FOR YOU MY ENTIRE LIFE"

E very minor act of kindness is valuable and precious. But every once in a while you will have an opportunity to say or do something for someone about which they will be able to say to you, "I've been waiting for you my entire life."

A tool for making a major difference in someone's life is to ask yourself, "What can I say or do for this person that will elicit his responding to me, "I've been waiting for you my entire life."?

- *I've heard a lot of criticism throughout my life. I've been waiting for someone to tell me that they see my good qualities and strengths.*
- *I have a serious learning disability. I've been waiting for someone to find a way to help me make a major breakthrough in my learning.*
- *I'm very sensitive to criticism and insults. I've been waiting*

for someone to help me feel so good about myself that I can view criticism and insults objectively without pain. I would love to be able to learn from valid comments and to be able to ignore those that are mistaken.

- *It's taking me a long time to find a suitable marriage partner. I've been waiting for someone to make the right suggestion.*
- *I feel that I have talents and skills that have not yet been utilized. I've been waiting for the right coach my whole life.*
- *I have accomplished a lot. But I feel that I could go much further if I were to have someone who could take care of the logistics for me.*
- *I desperately need to lose weight. I have tried many diets and many plans. So far nothing has worked for me. I can't do it alone. I need a coach who will stick with me while I experience my ups and downs.*
- *I don't experience very much joy in my life. Short lectures and books don't help me. I've been waiting for someone to train me to become more joyous. I need someone who will stick with me and reinforce the ideas I need to hear over and over again.*
- *I've been a doormat my entire life. I've been waiting for someone to teach me to speak up for myself.*
- *I feel discouraged about life. I've been waiting for someone to give me hope.*
- *I have always been indecisive. I've been waiting for someone to teach me to become more decisive.*
- *I have always been highly disorganized. I've been waiting*

for someone to help me become more organized.

- *I have always been fearful around other people. I've been waiting for someone to help me feel more comfortable.*
- *I have always lacked ambition. I've been waiting for someone to help me become more ambitious.*
- *I have always procrastinated. I'm waiting for someone to make me more proactive.*
- *I have always been waiting for someone to help me in some important way. But I don't even know what I am waiting for. I'm certain I'll recognize it when it happens. I am ultimately waiting for someone who knows me better than I know myself or at least who is aware of opportunities of which I am as yet unaware.*

CARRY ON KIND ACTS

L ist kind acts that other people have done for you that you can now do for others.

1. _____

2. _____

3. _____

4. _____

5. _____

6. _____

7. _____

8. _____

9. _____

10. _____

11. _____

12. _____

13. _____

14. _____

15. _____

16. _____

17. _____

18. _____

19. _____

20. _____

21. _____

22. _____

23. _____

24. _____

25. _____

26. _____